W9-AFT-763

NATURE

NATURE

POEMS OLD AND NEW

MAY
SWENSON

HOUGHTON MIFFLIN COMPANY

Boston   New York

1994

For information about permission to reproduce selections from this book, write to Permissions, Houghton Mifflin Company, 215 Park Avenue South, New York, New York 10003.

Library of Congress Cataloging-in-Publication Data

Swenson, May.
Nature : poems old and new / May Swenson.
p.   cm.
Includes index.
ISBN 0-395-69463-9 (cl.)   ISBN 0-395-69462-0 (pbk.)
I. Title.
PS3537.W4786N3   1994
811'.54—dc20   93-45642
CIP

Book design by Anne Chalmers

Printed in the United States of America

MP 10 9 8 7 6 5 4 3 2 1

The following poems are published for the first time: "Alternate Hosts," "The Fluffy Stuff," "Incantation," "Love Sleeping," "Lying and Looking," "Manyone Flying," "Once There Were Glaciers," "Skopus," "Subconscious Sea," "Yes, the Mystery."

Several poems previously appeared in the following publications: *Atlantic Monthly:* "The Snowy," "What I Did on a Rainy Day"; *Beloit Poetry Journal:* "A Tree in Spring"; *Chelsea:* "Picasso: 'Dream.' Oil. 1932"; *Lynx:* "As Long Ago As Far Away"; *The Nation:* "Horse," "Weather"; *The New Yorker:* "Last Day," "Look Closer," "Staring at the Sea on the Day of the Death of Another," "Stripping and Putting On"; *New York Times:* "Cabala"; *Orlando 3:* "Earth Your Dancing Place"; *Paris Review:* "Daffodildo"; *Poetry:* "The Sea"; *Poetry Northwest:* "My Farm"; *Saturday Review:* "Goodnight," "Haymaking." "Laocoön Dream Recorded in Diary Dated 1943" was published in a different form as "Riddle of One Hundred and One Rhymes" in *Springtime 3.*

"Comet Watch on Indian Key — Night of April 10, 1986," "Come In Go Out," "A Day Like Rousseau's *Dream,*" "Goodbye, Goldeneye," "If I Had

Children," "In the Bodies of Words," "A New Pair," "Summer's Bounty," and "Waterbird" previously appeared in *In Other Words* by May Swenson. Reprinted by permission of Alfred A. Knopf, Inc.

"After the Flight of Ranger 7," "At Truro," "Beginning to Squall," "By Morning," "Camoufleur," "Catbird in Redbud," "The Centaur," "The Cloud-Mobile," "Feel Like a Bird," "Flag of Summer," "Forest," "Fountain Piece," "Fountains of Aix," "Green Red Brown and White," "Hearing the Wind at Night," "Her Management," "How Everything Happens," "Living Tenderly," "Motherhood," "News from the Cabin," "Of Rounds," "Orbiter 5 Shows How Earth Looks from the Moon," "Out of the Sea, Early," "A Pair," "Question," "Rain at Wildwood," "Sleeping Overnight on the Shore," "The Stick," "Stone Gullets," "The Surface," "The Tide at Long Point," "Waking from a Nap on the Beach," "Water Picture," "The Wave and the Dune," and "The Woods at Night" previously appeared in *The Complete Poems to Solve* by May Swenson. Reprinted by permission of Macmillan Publishing Company. Fifteen lines of the second stanza of "The Truth Is Forced" were just published in *The Wonderful Pen of May Swenson*. Reprinted by permission of Macmillan Publishing Company.

"All That Time," "A Couple," "Early Morning: Cape Cod," "Evolution," "In the Yard," "A Loaf of Time," "Mornings Innocent," "One Morning in New Hampshire," "Secure," "Swimmers," "Untitled," "Wednesday at the Waldorf," and "The Willets" previously appeared in *The Love Poems of May Swenson*. "Beast," "Cumuli," and "A Day Is Laid By" are reprinted from *Another Animal* by May Swenson. "The Process" is reprinted from *A Cage of Spines* by May Swenson. "At First, at Last," "The Little Rapids," "Ocean Whale-Shaped," and "On Handling Some Small Shells from the Windward Islands" are reprinted from *Half Sun Half Sleep* by May Swenson. "*Spring* by Robert Lowell (Photograph by Trudi Fuller)" is reprinted from *Iconographs* by May Swenson. "The Alyscamps at Arles," "Another Spring Uncovered," "Big-Hipped Nature," "The Day Moon," "Downward," "Each Like a Leaf," "The Playhouse," "Sketch for a Landscape," "The Snow Geese at Jamaica Bay," "Sunday in the Country," and "Trinity Churchyard, Spring 1961" are reprinted from *To Mix with Time* by May Swenson. All other poems in this collection were previously published in *New and Selected Things Taking Place* by May Swenson.

Stanley Kunitz suggested this collection. Alice M. Geffen, J. C. Todd, and Lori Wood gave valuable advice. The poems were chosen and arranged by R. R. Knudson and Peter Davison, who dedicate *Nature* to the memory of three great friends of poetry: Marie Bullock, Betty Kray, and Howard Moss.

CONTENTS

FOREWORD, *by Susan Mitchell*

FRONTISPIECES

COME IN GO OUT · 3

LIVING TENDERLY · 3

UNTITLED · 4

A DAY IS LAID BY · 4

ON ITS WAY · 5

HOW TO BE OLD · 6

VIEW TO THE NORTH · 7

THE EXCHANGE · 8

SELVES

THE TRUTH IS FORCED · 11

A LAKE SCENE · 12

THE CENTAUR · 13

EARTH YOUR DANCING PLACE · 16

THE CROSSING · 17

THE POPLAR'S SHADOW · 18

I LOOK AT MY HAND · 19

IF I HAD CHILDREN · 20

A DREAM · 21

LAOCOÖN DREAM RECORDED
IN DIARY DATED 1943 · 22

CABALA · 23

SUNDAY IN THE COUNTRY · 24

BEAST · 25

MORNINGS INNOCENT · 26

EVOLUTION · 27

LOVE SLEEPING · 28

BLUE · 29

WHAT I DID ON A RAINY DAY · 30

LYING AND LOOKING · 30

ALMANAC · 31

GREEN RED BROWN AND WHITE · 32

A LOAF OF TIME · 33

FOREST · 34

THE THICKENING MAT · 35

DECIDING · 36

THE BEAUTY OF THE HEAD · 37

DAFFODILDO · 41

QUESTION · 45

BIRTHDAY · 45

ABOVE THE ARNO · 46

MANYONE FLYING · 49

THE LIGHTNING · 50

ON THE EDGE · 51

A SUBJECT OF THE WAVES · 52

AT TRURO · 54

OCTOBER · 55

DIGGING IN THE GARDEN OF AGE
I UNCOVER A LIVE ROOT · 60

THIS MORNING · 60

SCROPPO'S DOG · 61

HORSE · 63

BLEEDING · 64

HEARING THE WIND AT NIGHT · 65

THE FLUFFY STUFF · 65

WEATHER · 66

YES, THE MYSTERY · 67

THE LITTLE RAPIDS · 68

DOWNWARD · 68

SUBCONSCIOUS SEA · 69

RUSTY AUTUMN · 70

I WILL LIE DOWN · 71

SECURE · 71

STILL TURNING · 72

ORDER OF DIET · 74

THE ALYSCAMPS AT ARLES · 75

TRINITY CHURCHYARD, SPRING 1961 · 77

NATURE · 78

FEEL ME · 79

DEATH, GREAT SMOOTHENER · 80

LAST DAY · 81

THE ENGAGEMENT · 82

DAYS

A DAY LIKE ROUSSEAU'S *DREAM* · 85

SPRING UNCOVERED · 86

APRIL LIGHT · 87

A CITY GARDEN IN APRIL · 88

WATER PICTURE · 92

A TREE IN SPRING · 93

IN THE YARD · 94

RAIN AT WILDWOOD · 94

CATBIRD IN REDBUD · 96

SHU SWAMP, SPRING · 96

ONE MORNING IN NEW HAMPSHIRE · 97

SKETCH FOR A LANDSCAPE · 99

FLAG OF SUMMER · 100

HAYMAKING · 100

SUMMER'S BOUNTY · 102

HER MANAGEMENT · 102

FEATHERS

ON ADDY ROAD · 107

CAMOUFLEUR · 108

ANGELS AT "UNSUBDUED" · 108

THE WOODS AT NIGHT · 109

THE SNOWY · 110

FOUNTAIN PIECE · 112

THE SNOW GEESE AT JAMAICA BAY · 113

ONE OF THE STRANGEST · 113

PIGEON WOMAN · 114

A PAIR · 116

THE WILLETS · 117

GOODBYE, GOLDENEYE · 117

CAMPING IN MADERA CANYON · 118

ABOVE BEAR LAKE · 120

OCTOBER TEXTURES · 121

WATERBIRD · 122

A NEW PAIR · 122

ANOTHER SPRING UNCOVERED · 123

FEEL LIKE A BIRD · 124

STRIPPING AND PUTTING ON · 126

MAKINGS
❧

THE PLAYHOUSE · 131

DEAR ELIZABETH · 133

IN THE BODIES OF WORDS · 135

SPRING BY ROBERT LOWELL
(PHOTOGRAPH BY TRUDI FULLER) · 137

PICASSO: "DREAM." OIL. 1932 · 138

NAKED IN BORNEO · 138

MY FARM · 140

THE RED BIRD TAPESTRY · 141

DREAM AFTER NANOOK · 142

GOODNIGHT · 143

INSTINCTS
❧

NEWS FROM THE CABIN · 147

ALTERNATE HOSTS · 149

A COUPLE · 150

FABLE FOR WHEN THERE'S NO WAY OUT · 151

ZAMBESI AND RANEE · 152

BRONCO BUSTING, EVENT #1 · 154

MOTHERHOOD · 155

WEDNESDAY AT THE WALDORF · 157

BISON CROSSING NEAR MT. RUSHMORE · 158

DEATH INVITED · 158

BIG-HIPPED NATURE · 160

EACH LIKE A LEAF · 161

ALL THAT TIME · 163

OUT OF THE SEA, EARLY · 164

GODS | CHILDREN · 164

THE PROCESS · 168

HEAVENS

ONCE THERE WERE GLACIERS · 171

SLEEPING OVERNIGHT ON THE SHORE · 171

THE DAY MOON · 173

THE CLOUD-MOBILE · 174

CUMULI · 175

FLYING HOME FROM UTAH · 175

LANDING ON THE MOON · 177

ORBITER 5 SHOWS
HOW EARTH LOOKS FROM THE MOON · 178

AFTER THE FLIGHT OF RANGER 7 · 179

OF ROUNDS · 180

COMET WATCH ON INDIAN KEY
—NIGHT OF APRIL 10, 1986 · 182

SEEING JUPITER · 183

THE SOLAR CORONA · 184

AS LONG AGO AS FAR AWAY · 185

SKOPUS · 186

SURVEY OF THE WHOLE · 187

VISIONS

LOOK CLOSER · 191

A NAVAJO BLANKET · 192

BY MORNING · 193

THE NORTH RIM · 194

SPEED · 196

THE GARDEN AT ST. JOHN'S · 196

THE SURFACE · 198

ON HANDLING SOME SMALL SHELLS
FROM THE WINDWARD ISLANDS · 199

ANY OBJECT · 202

FOUNTAINS OF AIX · 203

WATERS

OCEAN, WHALE-SHAPED · 207

THE SEA · 208

FROM SEA CLIFF, MARCH · 209

STARING AT THE SEA ON THE
DAY OF THE DEATH OF ANOTHER · 210

THE PROMONTORY MOMENT · 210

EARLY MORNING: CAPE COD · 212

RUNNING ON THE SHORE · 213

CAPTAIN HOLM · 213

ST. AUGUSTINE-BY-THE-SEA · 214

XV

STONE GULLETS · 215

HOW EVERYTHING HAPPENS
(BASED ON A STUDY OF THE WAVE) · 216

AT FIRST, AT LAST · 217

SWIMMERS · 218

WAKING FROM A NAP ON THE BEACH · 219

BEGINNING TO SQUALL · 219

A HURRICANE AT SEA · 220

OLD NO. 1 · 222

ZERO IN THE COVE · 223

NOVEMBER NIGHT · 224

OVERBOARD · 225

THE WAVE AND THE DUNE · 226

THE BLUE BOTTLE · 227

THE STICK · 229

THE EVEN SEA · 230

THE TIDE AT LONG POINT · 230

AFTERPIECE

INCANTATION · 235

Index of Titles · 237

About the Poet · 241

FOREWORD

Susan Mitchell

"I hope they never get a rope on you, weather," May Swenson writes in one of her poems ("Weather"); "I hope they never put a bit in your mouth." My first response to these lines was, What a strange thing to say! And yet the feelings articulated are ones I recognize in myself: a love of the wild and the free, a joy in the still untamed.

What Swenson responds to and values in the world, its essential freedom, is the very quality that is most striking in her as a poet. When I read Swenson's poems, I feel that she is putting her face very close to the world, she has her cheek pressed against the tree she is looking at, her lips graze the petals of a flower she is admiring. "I put my nose into a fragrant/pompom, bite off some, and chew" ("Catbird in Redbud") — yes, for her, looking is an appetite; to see is to mouth the world, to glut and gorge. Or, as she puts it, "Now see,/seize with hasty sight" ("A Tree in Spring"), as if the whole world were fair prey and the poet enraptured were herself one of the raptors she frequently describes, the snowy owl, its "beak, like a third gleaming claw" ("The Snowy"), ready to grasp and devour.

Is it because Swenson looks with such attention at everything that the world appears strange in her poems? Or is it because she is attracted to the odd, the quirky, the idiosyncratic that she steps closer to savor a flamingo whose "split polished toe is mouth" and whose "rosy knee joints, bend/the wrong way" ("One of the Strangest") and to stare at the "pigeon woman" in front of the public library? She must have stared, and for a long time, to observe the woman's "plastic pink raincoat with a round/collar (looking like a little/girl) and flat gym shoes" and, especially marvelous, "her pimento-colored hair" ("Pigeon Woman"). Eyed by Swenson, the commonest things, what we all take for granted, like grass and rain, seem suddenly unprecedented and remarkable:

The rain fell like grass growing
upside down in the dark,
at first thin shoots,
short, crisp, far apart,

but, roots in the clouds,
a thick mat grew
quick, loquacious, lachrymose blades
blunt on the tent top.

("Rain at Wildwood")

O brave new world, I want to cry out, for no matter how unnatural the natural world appears in Swenson's poems, the strange does not leave me feeling estranged. This is a world looked at through love, through generosity of spirit. There is a largess to Swenson's vision; it is "big-hipped" like the Nature she wants to encompass in her poems. "Is Nature/this planet only? Or all the universe?" ("Nature"). For Swenson, the answer has to be "all the universe," from

A sprawled leaf, many-fingered, its radial
ridges limber, green — but curled,
tattered, pocked, the brown palm

nibbled by insects, nestled in by worms:
One leaf of a tree that's one tree of a forest,
that's the branch of the vein of a leaf

of a tree. Perpetual worlds
within, upon, above the world, the world
a leaf within a wilderness of worlds

("Flying Home from Utah")

to the moons that swirl around Jupiter in the chill of outer space:

Some small change
around it: three
little bits swirled,
or else my ragged eye

with wind swung.
In a black
pocket, behind
that blank, hung
hidden a fourth
moon dot; smarting
beneath my tongue,
dreg of ancient mint;
my retina tasted
light how long
dead?

("Seeing Jupiter")

Whether Swenson looks far in or far out in the universe she is in love with, Nature is teeming and packed with life, with textures, with tastes and smells, with "broken, rotting, shambled things" ("Her Management"). Though her poems are often compared with those of Dickinson, Bishop, and Moore because of her prodigious descriptive powers, her real kinship, I believe, is with Hopkins, another poet who looked closely at the world, another taster with an appetite for the overfull and the overcharged. Hopkins's vision of the world is as erotic as Swenson's, and if he had permitted himself to write about sexual desire, it would have been, I suspect, with Swenson's exuberant attention to detail:

I milknip your two Blue-skeined
blown Rose beauties, too, to sniff
their berries' blood, up stiff
pink tips. You're white in
patches, only mostly Rose,
buckskin and salty, speckled
like a sky. I love your spots,
your white neck, Rose, your hair's
wild straw splash, silk spools
for your ears.

("Blue")

Like Hopkins, Swenson takes pleasure in enumerating and listing, in rolling out the scrolls of Creation. To mouth is not only to take into the mouth but also to utter, to proclaim

> The brushy and hairy,
> tassely and slippery
>
> willow, fragmitie,
> cattail, goldenrod.
>
> The fluttery, whistley
> water-dimpling divers
>
> ("October Textures")

Though she does not share Hopkins's religious temperament, or, as she puts it in a long poem ("October"), "I do not mean to pray," she goes on to express her own version of gratitude for the grandeur and beauty of the dying season:

> But I am glad for the luck
> of light. Surely it is godly,
> that it makes all things
> begin, and appear, and become
> actual to each other.

To make the world actual is, of course, the poet's main business, and one way that Swenson accomplishes this is through metaphors that double and multiply whatever she turns her eye to. Describing small shells from the Windward Islands, Swenson, like the gypsy who made soup from a single rusty nail, evokes a world with sky and sunsets, with fish and birds:

> Some colored like flesh,
>
> > but more subtle than
> > corpuscle dyes. Some
>
> sunsets, some buttermilk
> skies, or penumbras

of moons in eclipse.
Malachite greens, fish-eyed

icy blues, pigeon-foot pinks,
brindled fulvous browns,

but most white like tektites.

("On Handling Some Small Shells
from the Windward Islands")

Any object can become an entry into a larger world, any one small piece or part of the whole evoke a universe. So experience is always complex, layered, laminated, with image superimposed on image, as if several slides had been simultaneously jammed into the projector. To tell the truth in a poem, Swenson must

say and cross out
and say over and say around
and say on top of and say in between
and say in symbol, in riddle,
in double meaning, under masks
of any feature, in the skins
of every creature.
And in my own skin, naked.

("The Truth Is Forced")

Metaphor is one way to "say on top of and say in between," one way to make the poem a horn of plenty equal to the world's plenitude — and to Swenson's. In a poem called "The Sea," she compares the smash of wave on shore to the breaking of a vase ("A monumental vase has broken on the beach"), but her own poem is like that monumental vase:

When the sea is calm I wade
into her glossy swells
Their bloom of froth sways toward me
Like crossing a field where the grain
ripens ever higher
I would walk to the true center

leaving no furrow behind me
would walk down
in the secret shade
and hide like a child
by the motionless roots
of the tall tangled water

At one and the same time, I enter the ocean and a field of grain, I am in the present and in the past, I am adult and child. As I wade into this passage, I witness a transformation: in some magical way, the water has grown as tall as grain and become a tangle of roots. But isn't experience always this tangled? And isn't that precisely why it is so difficult to speak of the moments that affect us most powerfully? In the imagination, the senses fuse, they penetrate one another like rocks that become molten when subjected to tremendous heat and pressure — or at least, this is what happens in the imagination of a great poet:

Flowers are shrieks of color
in the gullies, are shaped to leap or fly, some with
sharp orange beaks or curved purple necks, or they
thrust out vermilion tongues. Velvet clubs, jeweled
ships, silky whisks and puffs and beaded clusters
combine their freakish perfumes.

("A Day Like Rousseau's *Dream*")

The world that Swenson inhabits is finally the world of her own imagination, which is to say it is our world intensified, pitched an octave higher. Still, her imagination was fed and nurtured by what Shakespeare would have called the "material sap," a sensuous real that she is always trying to get back to and immerse herself in:

When I was a sea worm
I never saw the sun,

but flowed, a salty germ,
in the bloodstream of the sea.

("At Truro")

Even her individuality, her quirkiness, do not keep her from feeling one with the rest of humanity. Though she is the bird that flies on the edge of the flock, where there is "time to think, space to feel/private in" ("Manyone Flying"), she is not lonely because she is not one only — she is Manyone.

FRONTISPIECES

COME IN GO OUT

COME IN	GO OUT
A world of storm	A life of waves
Raging circles form	Tides and icy caves
Wind loops the globe	Sun scorching palms
Blizzards in the brain	Or deadening calms
Then modifying hope	A single summer day
A hoisted sail	Unfolds twinkling
On the dream trail	Flinches past the eye
Hummingbird's green	Bullet of gauze
Illuminant	Of primal cause

LIVING TENDERLY

My body a rounded stone
with a pattern of smooth seams.
My head a short snake,
retractive, projective.
My legs come out of their sleeves
or shrink within,
and so does my chin.
My eyelids are quick clamps.

My back is my roof.
I am always at home.

I travel where my house walks.
It is a smooth stone.
It floats within the lake,
or rests in the dust.
My flesh lives tenderly
inside its bone.

UNTITLED

I   will   be   earth   you   be   the   flower
You   have   found   my   root   you   are   the   rain
I   will   be   boat   and   you   the   rower
You   rock   you   toss   me   you   are   the   sea
How   be   steady   earth   that's   now   a   flood
The   root's   the   oar's   afloat   where's   blown   our   bud
We   will   be   desert   pure   salt   the   seed
Burn   radiant   sex   born   scorpion   need

A DAY IS LAID BY

A day is laid by
It came to pass
Wind is drained
from the willow

Dusk interlaces
the grass
Out of the husk
of twilight
emerges the moon

This the aftermath
of jaded sunset

of noon
and the sirens of bees

Day and wrath
are faded
Now above the bars
of lonely pastures
loom the sacred stars

ON ITS WAY

Orange on its way to ash,
Anger that a night will quench.

Passion in its honey swell
Pumpkin-plump before the rot.

Bush of fire everywhere,
Fur of hillside running flame.

Rush of heat to rosehip cheek,
Ripeness on its way to frost.

Glare of blood before the black.
Foxquick pulse. The sun a den.

Heartkill, and the gold a gun.
It is death that taints the leaves.

HOW TO BE OLD

It is easy to be young. (Everybody is,
at first.) It is not easy
to be old. It takes time.
Youth is given; age is achieved.
One must work a magic to mix with time
in order to become old.

Youth is given. One must put it away
like a doll in a closet,
take it out and play with it only
on holidays. One must have many dresses
and dress the doll impeccably
(but not to show the doll, to keep it hidden).

It is necessary to adore the doll,
to remember it in the dark on the ordinary
days, and every day congratulate
one's aging face in the mirror.

In time one will be very old.
In time, one's life will be accomplished.
And in time, in time, the doll —
like new, though ancient — will be found.

VIEW TO THE NORTH

As you grow older, it gets colder.
You see through things.
I'm looking through the trees,

their torn and thinning leaves,
to where chill blue water
is roughened by wind.

Day by day the scene opens,
enlarges, rips of space
appear where full branches

used to snug the view.
Soon it will be wide, stripped,
entirely unobstructed:

I'll see right through
the twining waves, to
the white horizon, to the place

where the North begins.
Magnificent! I'll be thinking
while my eyeballs freeze.

THE EXCHANGE

Now my body flat,
the ground breathes.
I'll be the grass.

Populous and mixed is mind.
Earth, take thought.
My mouth, be moss.

Field, go walking.
I, a disk,
will look down with seeming eye.

I will be time
and study to be evening.
You world, be clock.

I will stand,
a tree here,
never to know another spot.

Wind, be motion.
Birds, be passion.
Water, invite me to your bed.

SELVES

THE TRUTH IS FORCED

Not able to be honest in person
I wish to be honest in poetry.
Speaking to you, eye to eye, I lie
because I cannot bear
to be conspicuous with the truth.
Saying it — all of it — would be
taking off my clothes.
I would forfeit my most precious properties:
distance, secrecy, privacy.
I would be exposed. And I would be
possessed. It would be an entire
surrender (to you, eye to eye).
You would examine me too closely.
You would handle me.
All your eyes would swarm me.
I'd be forever after hotly dressed
in your cloying, itching, greedy bees.
Whether you are one or two or many
it is the same. Really, I feel as if
one pair of eyes were a whole hive.
So I lie (eye to eye)
by leaving the core of things unvoiced
or else by offering a dummy
in place of myself.

One must be honest somewhere. I wish
to be honest in poetry.
With the written word.
Where I can say and cross out

and say over and say around
and say on top of and say in between
and say in symbol, in riddle,
in double meaning, under masks
of any feature, in the skins
of every creature.
And in my own skin, naked.
I am glad, indeed I dearly crave
to become naked in poetry,
to force the truth
through a poem,
which, when it is made, if real,
not a dummy, tells me
and then you (all or any, eye to eye)
my whole self,
the truth.

A LAKE SCENE

So innocent this scene, I feel I see it
    with a deer's eye,
uncovering a first secret from this shore.
    I think of the smoothest thing:
the inside of a young thigh,
    or the line of a torso when, supine,
the pectoral sheath crosses the armpit
    to the outflung arm;
at the juncture of lake and hills, that zone,
    the lowest hill in weavings
of fainter others overlaid,
    is a pelvis in shadow.

The hazel waves slip toward me,
    the far arcade
honed by the sunset; nothing tears
    the transparent skin that water

and sky and, between them,
    the undulant horizon wears.
No contest here, no roughness,
    no threat,
the wind's lick mild as the lake's,
    the rock I lean on, moss-round
as that silhouette
    in the thwart of the opposite shore;
spruce and fir snug-wool its folds.

    My eye goes there, to the source
of a first secret. I would be inheritor
    of the lamb's way and the deer's,
my thrust take from the ground
    I tread or lie on. In thighs of trees,
in recumbent stones, in the loins
    of beasts is found
that line my own nakedness carried.
    Here, in an Eden of the mind,
I would remain among my kind,
    to lake and hill, to tree and beast married.

THE CENTAUR

The summer that I was ten —
Can it be there was only one
summer that I was ten? It must

have been a long one then —
each day I'd go out to choose
a fresh horse from my stable

which was a willow grove
down by the old canal.
I'd go on my two bare feet.

But when, with my brother's jack-knife,
I had cut me a long limber horse
with a good thick knob for a head,

and peeled him slick and clean
except a few leaves for the tail,
and cinched my brother's belt

around his head for a rein,
I'd straddle and canter him fast
up the grass bank to the path,

trot along in the lovely dust
that talcumed over his hoofs,
hiding my toes, and turning

his feet to swift half-moons.
The willow knob with the strap
jouncing between my thighs

was the pommel and yet the poll
of my nickering pony's head.
My head and my neck were mine,

yet they were shaped like a horse.
My hair flopped to the side
like the mane of a horse in the wind.

My forelock swung in my eyes,
my neck arched and I snorted.
I shied and skittered and reared,

stopped and raised my knees,
pawed at the ground and quivered.
My teeth bared as we wheeled

and swished through the dust again.
I was the horse and the rider,
and the leather I slapped to his rump

spanked my own behind.
Doubled, my two hoofs beat
a gallop along the bank,

the wind twanged in my mane,
my mouth squared to the bit.
And yet I sat on my steed

quiet, negligent riding,
my toes standing the stirrups,
my thighs hugging his ribs.

At a walk we drew up to the porch.
I tethered him to a paling.
Dismounting, I smoothed my skirt

and entered the dusky hall.
My feet on the clean linoleum
left ghostly toes in the hall.

Where have you been? said my mother.
Been riding, I said from the sink,
and filled me a glass of water.

What's that in your pocket? she said.
Just my knife. It weighted my pocket
and stretched my dress awry.

Go tie back your hair, said my mother,
and *Why is your mouth all green?*
*Rob Roy, he pulled some clover
as we crossed the field,* I told her.

EARTH YOUR DANCING PLACE

Beneath heaven's vault
remember always walking
through halls of cloud
down aisles of sunlight
or through high hedges
of the green rain
walk in the world
highheeled with swirl of cape
hand at the swordhilt
of your pride
Keep a tall throat
Remain aghast at life

Enter each day
as upon a stage
lighted and waiting
for your step
Crave upward as flame
have keenness in the nostril
Give your eyes
to agony or rapture

Train your hands
as birds to be
brooding or nimble
Move your body
as the horses
sweeping on slender hooves
over crag and prairie
with fleeing manes
and aloofness of their limbs

Take earth for your own large room
and the floor of earth
carpeted with sunlight
and hung round with silver wind
for your dancing place

THE CROSSING

With stealthy whistle of wing
the hawk crossed over
the very air I breathed
and sank in some cover.
Through water where I drank
the deer stepped slow
without chinking a stone
and slid into shadow.

The mountain's body ahead,
the same heaving ground
I walked, hurried up
and out, away, and around
to where the distance stood.
That could not flee or hide.
It filled me. I filled it
and was satisfied.

THE POPLAR'S SHADOW

When I was little, when
the poplar was in leaf,
its shadow made a sheaf,
the quill of a great pen
dark upon the lawn
where I used to play.

Grown, and long away
into the city gone,
I see the pigeons print
a loop in air and, all
their wings reversing, fall
with silver undertint
like poplar leaves, their seams
in the wind blown.

Time's other side, shown
as a flipped coin, gleams
on city ground
when I see a pigeon's feather:
little and large together,
the poplar's shadow is found.

Staring at here,
and superposing then,
I wait for when.
What shapes will appear?
Will great birds swing
over me like gongs?
The poplar plume belongs
to what enormous wing?

I LOOK AT MY HAND

I look at my hand and see
  it is also his and hers;
the pads of the fingers his,

      the wrists and knuckles hers.
      In the mirror my pugnacious eye
      and ear of an elf, his;

        my tamer mouth and slant
            cheekbones hers.
      His impulses my senses swarm,
    her hesitations they gather.
      Father and Mother
      who dropped me,

    an acorn in the wood,
    repository of your shapes
  and inner streams and circles,

  you who lengthen toward heaven,
forgive me
    that I do not throw

the replacing green
  trunk when you are ash.
  When you are ash, no
features shall there be,
tangled of you,
  interlacing hands and faces

  through me
who hide, still hard,
  far down under your shades —

      and break my root, and prune my buds,
        that what can make no replica
    may spring from me.

IF I HAD CHILDREN

If I had children, I might name
them astrometeorological names:
Meridian, a girl. Zenith, a boy.
Eclipse, a pretty name for either one.
Anaximander, ancient Greek scientist
(who built a gnomon on Lacedaemon,
and with it predicted the exact date

that city would be destroyed by
earthquake). . . . Anaximander, wonderful
name for a girl. Anny could be her
nickname. Ion, short for ionosphere,
would make a graceful name for
a boy. Twins could be named after
planets: Venus and Mercury, or

Neptune and Mars. They'd adore each
other's heavenly bodies shining
upon their doubles on Earth.
And have you ever thought that, of
the Nine, only one planet is female?
Venus. Unless Earth is. So, seven
of Sun's children, it seems, are male.

But, if I had children, and grandchild-
ren, then greatgrandchildren, myriads
of newborn moons and moonlets crowding
into the viewfinder would furnish me
names both handsome and sweet:
Phoebe, Rhea, Dione among daughters
of Saturn, with Titan and Janus the

brothers. Io, Ganymede and Callisto,
Jupiter's boys: Europa and little
Amalthea, their sisters.
On Io, most exotic of the Galilean

moons, are mapped six great-and-grand
volcanoes: Loki, Hemo, Horus, Daedalus,
Tarsis, Ra. Beauties all! But all

boys. Well, if I had children
I wouldn't fix genders or orbits, only
names for them. Wobbling Phobus,
distant child of Mars, misshapen as
a frozen potato. . . . If I had such a
lopsided moon, the name Phobus would
fit. And I'd love it just the same.

A DREAM

I was a god and self-enchanted
I stood in a cabinet in the living wood
The doors were carved with the sign of the lizard
whose eye unblinks on emptiness
whose head turns slower than a tooth grows

I wore a mask of skin-thin silver
My hair was frenzied foam stiffened to ice
My feet gloved in petals of imperishable flowers
were hooves and colder than hammers

I lived by magic
A little bag in my chest held a whirling stone
so hot it was past burning
so radiant it was blinding

When the moon rose worn and broken
her face like a coin endlessly exchanged
in the hands of the sea
her ray fell upon the doors which opened
and I walked in the living wood
The leaves turned bronze and the moss to marble

At morning I came back to my cabinet
It was a tree in the daylight
the lizard a scroll of its bark

LAOCOÖN DREAM RECORDED IN DIARY DATED 1943

In half-sleep felt an arm go round me,
but longer than an arm, it lapped me twice
and I was bound, but did not mind.
One supple coil lay nice about my waist
without alarm and, skilled and strong,
the other winding cool and careful, slipped
to my hip, tightening without haste.
An odd thrill made a geyser in my blood.
This love had a new taste.

Now the arms were three, all slick
along my nakedness, and thick.
A fourth, more slender, hugged my thigh.
I did not wake. Dream-submerged
as in a tepid lake, I lay, postponing fear.
A quick and tender tongue flicked at my neck,
groped higher, licked into my ear.
Below I felt each toe receive a velvet ring,
and soon there sat around my ankles
worm-wet bracelets, fat and glistening.

Cap-eyed, caressed all ways at once,
I did not care to identify my lover, nor dare
apprise him by a finger-try. My hands
crept to my head. A thousand tousled vipers
rippled there, from braid and curlicue
had made their lair. With lips of suede
they grazed upon my brows, breathed hissing
kisses to my mouth and, seething, sipped

my nipples, where mini-eels, each narrow
as a hair, sprouted in a copious stream.

Roused, I could not rise. Anger and desire
were one. A ton of horror poured an equal
weight of lust, of drowsy hate, of heavy
bliss like a drug upon my dream.
The five arms held me snug.
Roped by a riddle in spiral shape
in a lunar nightmare I was ready for rape.

A gentle murderer whose many-stranded will
never could be severed, nor a motive in the kill
unraveled, the six arms traveled me entire,
and trussed me heel to nape.
I, the victim recognizing all my strangled
cries as lies, my tangled fears as wishes
in disguise, snatched the seventh arm,
greater than the rest, with both my own
and pressed it close. Its wide girth
matched my chest. Its voracious face,
the jaws agape, avid on the vipers fed.
Into that hollow my head was swallowed, open-eyed.
The dream was done, so there was no escape.

CABALA

I will turn very dark,
dark as an idol
in a shady room.
And be his eye, alive
because he is so still.

Or I will turn
dark as a horse
across a burnished pasture

in the shade of a tree.
There I will be

the star on his brow, so still.
Dark as a target,
and as the flint
behind the white feather,
a mark that does not move

to draw all shafts.
Eye light and mind light,
lightning-taming leather
I will turn and be
a swiftness on the dark.

SUNDAY IN THE COUNTRY

No wind-wakeness here. A cricket's creed
intoned to the attentive wood all day.
The sun's incessant blessing. Too much gold
weighs on my head where I lay it in light.
Angels climb through my lashes, their wings
so white, every color clings there. Sky,
deep and accusing in its blue, scrapes
my conscience like a nail. I'm glad
for the gray spider who, with torpid
menace, mounts my shoe; for the skittish
fly with his green ass and orange eyes,
who wades in hairs of my arm to tickle
his belly. Long grass, silky as a monk's
beard, the blades all yellow-beamed.
Corporeal self's too shapeful for this manger.
I'm mesmerized by trumpet sun
funneling hallelujah to my veins.

Until, at the tabernacle's back, a blurt
guffaw is heard. An atheistic stranger calls

a shocking word. That wakes the insurrection!
Wind starts in the wood, and strips the pompous
cassocks from the pines. A black and
impudent Voltairean crow has spoiled
the sacrament. And I can rise and go.

BEAST

my Brown self
goes on four paws
supple-twining in the
lewd Gloom

arching against the
shaggy hedges
with a relishing Purr
tasting among his
spurted fur

the Ripeness
brisk and willing
of his brown body

yawning Obscurely
glittered-glancing
couching himself
in the sunny places

beating his tail
where traces
of She-odor make
a pattern for
his unbrained thought

feeling the Budding
thorns in his
feet of felt

planning to Stab them
into the wincing pelt
of a creature smaller

my Brown self
a thing gleam-jawed
goes downright
Four-pawed

MORNINGS INNOCENT

I wear your smile upon my lips
arising on mornings innocent
Your laughter overflows my throat
Your skin is a fleece about me
With your princely walk I salute the sun
People say I am handsome

Arising on mornings innocent
birds make the sound of kisses
Leaves flicker light and dark like eyes

I melt beneath the magnet of your gaze
Your husky breath insinuates my ear
Alert and fresh as grass I wake

and rise on mornings innocent
The strands of the wrestler
run golden through my limbs
I cleave the air with insolent ease
With your princely walk I salute the sun
People say I am handsome

EVOLUTION

the stone
would like to be
Alive like me

the rooted tree
longs to be Free

the mute beast
envies my fate
Articulate

on this ball
half dark
half light
i walk Upright
i lie prone
within the night

beautiful each Shape
to see
wonderful each Thing
to name
here a stone
there a tree
here a river
there a Flame

marvelous to Stroke
the patient beasts
within their yoke

how i Yearn
for the lion
in his den
though he spurn
the touch of men

the longing
that i know
is in the Stone also
it must be

the same that rises
in the Tree
the longing
in the Lion's call
speaks for all

oh to Endure
like the stone
sufficient
to itself alone

or Reincarnate
like the tree
be born each spring
to greenery

or like the lion
without law
to roam the Wild
on velvet paw

but if walking
i meet
a Creature like me
on the street
two-legged
with human face
to recognize
is to Embrace

wonders pale
beauties dim
during my delight
with Him

an Evolution strange
two Tongues touch
exchange
a Feast unknown
to stone
or tree or beast

LOVE SLEEPING

Life in the throat of my love leaps
though love is sleeping
under the eyelids of my love Look
a dream is darting
as the blood darts in the throat's vein
and love's shoulder warms my cheek
a dream floats to my love's brain

Heart in the chest of my love moves
though sleeping proving
the flesh of love will wake See
a breath is taken
as a dream makes the brow of my love smile
and the face's flower and the hair's leaves
quiver in a wind of love on that isle

where the heart beats now Watch
I will watch for the meeting
of my love with love in the heat
of the dream's full quaking
as love's body wakes in my arms' catch
and life in my chest and throat leaps
though love is sleeping

BLUE

Blue, but you are Rose, too,
and buttermilk, but with blood
dots showing through.
A little salty your white
nape boy-wide. Glinting hairs
shoot back of your ears' Rose
that tongue likes to feel
the maze of, slip into the funnel,
tell a thunder-whisper to.
When I kiss, your eyes' straight
lashes down crisp go like doll's
blond straws. Glazed iris Roses,
your lids unclose to Blue-ringed
targets, their dark sheen-spokes
almost green. I sink in Blue-
black Rose-heart holes until you
blink. Pink lips, the serrate
folds taste smooth, and Rosehip-
round, the center bud I suck.
I milknip your two Blue-skeined
blown Rose beauties, too, to sniff
their berries' blood, up stiff
pink tips. You're white in
patches, only mostly Rose,
buckskin and salty, speckled
like a sky. I love your spots,
your white neck, Rose, your hair's
wild straw splash, silk spools
for your ears. But where white
spouts out, spills on your brow
to clear eyepools, wheel shafts
of light, Rose, you are Blue.

WHAT I DID ON A RAINY DAY

Breathed the fog from the valley
Inhaled its ether fumes
With whittling eyes peeled the hills
to their own blue and bone
Swallowed piercing pellets of rain
Caught cloudsful in one colorless cup
Exhaling stung the earth with sunlight
Struck leaf and bristle to green fire
Turned tree trunks to gleaming pillars
and twigs to golden nails
With one breath taken into the coils
of my blood and given again when vibrant
I showed who's god around here

LYING AND LOOKING

The way
the hairs grow
on my skin,
I see they
glisten.
Furrowed
as by wind,
my armpits
are fleecy pods;
my grassy skin's
darker in folds
of elbow and groin
and kneecap dents;
if I stretch my legs
each knee's a face
square-cheeked, pugnacious.
My thighs dip and play
in glossy light;

their backs stay
level, though they
arch and roll; panther-
colored, between buff
and peach, soft
but chamois-tough;
and slanting
curiously
from alert pores,
their hairs
are blond. Oh, I
wouldn't trade my
body for anything. Not
for a dove's white boat,
not for a bear's black coat,
not for anything.

ALMANAC

The hammer struck my nail, instead of nail.
A moon flinched into being. Omen-black,
it began its trail. Risen from horizon
on my thumb (no longer numb and indigo)
it waxed yellow, waned to a sliver that now
sets white, here at the rim I cut tonight.

I make it disappear, but mark its voyage
over my little oval ceiling that again
is cloudless, pink and clear. In the dark
quarter-inch of this moon before it arrived
at my nail's tip, an unmanned airship
dived 200 miles to the hem of space, and
vanished. At the place of Pharaoh Cheops'
tomb (my full moon floating yellow)
a boat for ferrying souls to the sun
was disclosed in a room sealed 5000 years.

Reaching whiteness, this moon-speck waned
while an April rained. Across the street,
a vine crept over brick up 14 feet. And
Einstein (who said there is no hitching
post in the universe) at 77 turned ghost.

GREEN RED BROWN AND WHITE

Bit an apple on its red
side   Smelled like snow
Between white halves broken open
brown winks slept in sockets of green

Stroked a birch white as a thigh
scar-flecked smooth as the neck
of a horse   On mossy pallets green
the pines dropped down
their perfect carvings brown

Lost in the hairy wood
followed berries red
to the fork   Had to choose
between green and green   High

in a sunwhite dome a brown bird
sneezed   Took the path least likely
and it led me home   For

each path leads both out and in
I come while going   No to and from
There is only here   And here
is as well as there   Wherever
I am led I move within the care
of the season
hidden in the creases of her skirts
of green or brown or beaded red

And when they are white
I am not lost   I am not lost then
only covered for the night

A LOAF OF TIME

A loaf of time
round and thick
So many layers
ledges to climb
to lie on our
bellies lolling
licking our lips
The long gaze a
gull falling
down the cliff's
table   to coast
the constant
waves   The reach-
ing wave-tongues
lick the table
But slowly grayly
slow as the ocean
is gray beyond
the green   slow
as the sky is high
and out of sight
higher than blue
is white   Around
the table's wheel
unbounded   for
each a meal the
centered mound to
be divided   A
wedge for each
and leisure on

                        each ledge   The
                     round loaf thick
                     we lick our lips
                         Our eyes gull
                     down the layered
                          cliff and ride
                     the reaching waves
        that lick but   slowly
                             the table's
        edge   Then slowly
           our loaf   Slowly
                          our ledge

FOREST

The pines, aggressive as erect tails of cats,
bob their tips when the wind freshens.

An alert breath like purring stirs below,
where I move timid over humps of hair,

crisp, shadow-brindled, heaving as if
exhilarated muscular backs felt

the wisps of my walking. Looking to sky,
glaring then closing between the slow

lashes of boughs, I feel observed:
up high are oblong eyes that know,

as their slits of green light
expand, squeeze shut, expand,

that I stand here. Suddenly I go,
flick-eyed, hurrying over fur

needles that whisper as if they weren't dead.
My neck-hairs rise. The feline forest grins

behind me. Is it about to follow?
Which way out through all these whiskered yawns?

THE THICKENING MAT

My track the first
on new snow:
each step, with soft
snap, pressed
a padded button
into a thickening
mat — snug sensation,
satisfying pattern —
to the corner,
where I turned and

met the wind:
whips to my eyes
and mouth. This way
all I breathe
is snow. Marks
of my feet, unique,
black-edged under
the streetlight —
where are they?
All blank, all white.

DECIDING

Deciding to go on digging doing it
what they said outside wasn't any use
Inside hiding it made it get ambitious
Like a potato in a dark bin
it grew white grabbers for light
out of its navel eyes not priding
itself much just deciding
it wasn't true inside what they said
outside those bumps were

All humped alike dumped inside
slumped in burlap said
roots are no good out of ground
a fruit's crazy to want to be a flower
Besides it's sin changing the given shape
Bursting the old brown skin is suicide
Wishing to taste like a tulip
sip colored light
outside thumps said isn't right

Deciding to keep on striding
from inside bursting the bin-side
poking out wishes for delicious opposites
turning blind eyes to strong fingers
touching meaning more than sight
the navel scars of weaning
used for something finally
Deciding to go on digging doing it

THE BEAUTY OF THE HEAD

Shuswap River, Sicamous, B.C.

I

Black bear, pacing the shore, lollops over
a fallen pine. Loon in the swampy inlet lets go
his weird choked cry. Bowl of the lake rocks,
dinghy at the stern champs-stammers. Waves slosh,
my mouth waters, my ear's cochlea fills up,
and empties. I notice how I breathe,
in the cradle of my ribs, to the shift of the lake.
Violet-green swallows slant-fall to a field
of Alpine flowers, where sparse, far-apart blue
wicks, red brushpoints, wink in the moraine.
At night, on the mountain's shoulder pied with
snow, glints the lit hut of a star.
Where we dock this evening, two red-necked
grebe and a loon work their waterlily acre,
dive in turn, and reproject the trumpets
of their necks. Breaking the surface, they break
silence, slip west, silver the last light.
We'll sleep on deck, topside the houseboat,
slap mosquitoes, but first, roast chub
in a flat-stone oven dug on the shore.
These stones, all for skipping, whittled by the lake,
were hot shingles we lay on in sunlight,
drying our hair. Lake is our bathtub, dish-sink,
drinking jug, and (since the boat's head doesn't work,
— the ice box, either — the bilge pump barely)
lake is water closet, too. Little I knew
a gale this night would wash, and then
wind-wipe my rump hung over the rail.

Black bear straddles the log he rolled off,
lopes to the lake, wades in a ways, and sips,
lips making a ripple. He lies down like a dog
in the soft silt, then, up with a lurch, he exits.
Bush of the bank closes around his haunches.
Uneasy, I scan the dusky beach. Is he that hole
in the end of a log in the sunset? — that root
of a cottonwood stump? — that near shadow
dilating, indenting the bush?
As wind rises, tide rises. Moon swings out —
anchor that can't catch — and wanders half-circle.
We lie in our sacks, clouds and the mountain
traveling, woods and waves exchanging
horizons, dipping, carousing. We mummy-sacks sway
with the deck. Tied up on a long line to a pine,
the bow starts to strain, stomp, scrape
on shore stones. Aft pushed broadside, the boat is about
to be grounded, while with each ram of rising water,
the dinghy knocks, bucks, whines to mount
the stern. No running lights on the *Alice B.*,
and, its battery weak, the flashlight's beam
has no reach. It's our second mooring.
First night in the river's mouth was calm.
Now, water hard as walls shoves starboard,
wants to fling the boat on a shelf
of ripping, skipping rocks — the first, then the second
shelf — the third would set it next the pines
by morning, low tide leave it really a house
on land. And, in the middle of this
bouncing, howling lake-quake, I have to go.
Backing down the deck ladder is one thing,
perching on the teetering rail (away from portside
where Skipper and Mates are bunked) is another,

hanging on and hanging *out,* in the lurch and clamor —
not minding the dunk, but hoping not to fall
overboard, while going — is toughest of all.
I succeed and, backside baptized, feel
a mariner's talent proved.

3

Three A.M. By four it will be light.
No one nervous but me, the other three asleep.
Bedded down on the bench in the stern,
keeping watch, kept soaked ritualistically
by wave spray, I check the bilge by the dirty
eye of the lamp. Yes, the lake is leaking
to the deck. But, as if mine had pacified it,
big water eases, groans of boat and dinghy
come gradually to cease.
Meaning greater danger? Half the house has climbed
the beach. Unless got under way with the tide high,
here's where we'll stay. So I wake First Mate
and make such a nag it wakes Skipper.
With dawn, the engine started, anchor up, we untie
and, bup-bup-bup, we're off, open throttle
into the wind, over the smacking lake.
Mosquitoes blow off, sun peeps over the mountain.
Wet, ensacked, exhausted I crimp
in the galley-bunk to sleep.

My face a knot
became in sleep.
Anxiety and storm.
Confusion.
Not only was my
ground a wave,
but wrestling waves
deformed that wave.
My thoughts were torn,
my hipbones had no rest,
and I was clenched.
Darkness that strangles,
thrashing noise,
the source unknown.
Threat of being smashed
at bottom of a hole —
the cave of a huge,
insane, conglomerating
wave. And sun whipped
my glued eyelids.

Waked, I stood
at the point of the prow,
looking down into clear
water, like a well,
in still mountain shadow.
Anchor twinkled far below
in a slot between
humped stones,
smooth as glass,
where soft-nosed fish
lay moveless, but
for sideways flicks
of their circular eyes.
Boat rocking gently,
tethered to shore.
Brushing my body,
the early wind,
redolent of pine,
freshened and loosened
my forehead.

5

Tonight we are docked at the top of the lake's
right arm, at a fisherman's inn, awaiting dinner
around a thick oak table. In the window frame,
a crook-treed orchard where a blond horse crops
the flowing grass. A woman, in a wind-torn dress,
brings a full bucket to the buckskin. We play chess
and drink the stinging beer,
while our fish fries in the kitchen.
All secure, on shore for the night, the *Alice B.*,
snugged tight to an iron bust on the pier.
When, squint-eyed from the flashing river,
we climbed into farmyard shade, I spied
the squeaking door of a little privy

of new pine board, among trees beyond
where the blond horse crops. The bright
hook worked like silk. One seat, and no wasps,
it was all mine. An almanac, the pages Bible-thin,
hung by a string through a hole made with an awl.
Outside, steady silence, and in
the slit-moon-window, high up, a fragrant
tassel of pine. Alone, at peace, and journey done,
I sat. Feet planted on dependable planks, I sat.
Engrossed by the beauty of knothole panel before me,
I sat a nice long time.

DAFFODILDO

A daffodil from Emily's lot
I lay beside her headstone
on the first day of May.
I brought
another with me, threaded
through my buttonhole, the spawn
of ancestor she planted
where, today,
I trod her lawn.
A yellow small decanter
of her perfume, hermit-wild
and without a stopper,
next to her stone I filed
to give her back her property —
it's well it cannot spill.
Lolling on my jacket,
Emily's other daffodil.

Now, rocking to the racket
of the train, I try
recalling all her parlor's
penetration of my eye,

remembering mainly spartan
sunlight through the dimity
of the window-bay, evoking
her white-dressed anonymity.
    I remember, as if spoken
in my head: "I'm
nobody! Who
are you?"
thinking
how liked by time
she still is. It has linked
the hemlocks closer in their
hedge so that her privacy
remains. A denser lair,
in fact, than when she was alive
and looked through that bay
on the long garden
where I looked today.

    Another lady is its warden
now. She smells like bread
and butter. A New England pug-
face, she's eighty-seven, may be dead
before another host of plugless
yellow daintycups
springs next spring in the grass.
(What if one white bulb still sups
sun-time that Emily's shoe passed
over?) That old
black-dressed lady told
me, "Here's where
she soaked her gowns in this square
copper boiler on hot bricks." Whiteness
takes much washing. "Oh, her chair,"
she said, suddenly sprightly,
leading me up the stair
to a blue bedroom. "Mustn't forget to
show you

that. It's stored
in a closet." She brought out
a seat for a four-
year-old, only the cane devoutly
replaced, the ladderback and
legs of cherrywood original.
"An awe came on the trinket,"
one article her hand
would have known all
its life.

   "Geneva's farthest skill,"
I pondered,
"can't put the puppet
bowing," and retrieved
an answer,
   "I dwell
in Possibility —
a fairer
house than Prose." Yellow
bells in the still
air of their green room
out there
under the upstairs window
mutely swung.
   Shining through their cups,
her sunny ghost
passed down the rows.
"A word is dead
when it is said,
some say.
I say
it just begins to live that day."

   To her headstone I walked uphill.
It stands white without arrogance
on a green plot
that is her myth-filled

lot
now. Almost blank. Relatives
shoulder her in a straight rank.
Emily, 130 years older
since you took your
little throne
when you were four,
I crane
but can never
gain
that high chair
where you will ever
sit! Alone.

Self-confessed, and rocking
to the racket of the train,
I play back how
I picked you for my pocket,
stooped at your plain
stone.
    One gold dildo
I leave you from the host
I stole;
the other, holy,
I will keep until
it shrinks to ghost.
    "Disdaining men,
and oxygen,"
your grassy
breast I kiss
and make
this vow, Emily, to "take
vaster
attitudes — and strut upon my stem."

QUESTION

Body my house
my horse my hound
what will I do
when you are fallen

Where will I sleep
How will I ride
What will I hunt

Where can I go
without my mount
all eager and quick
How will I know
in thicket ahead
is danger or treasure
when Body my good
bright dog is dead

How will it be
to lie in the sky
without roof or door
and wind for an eye

With cloud for shift
how will I hide?

BIRTHDAY

What am I doing here?
What are the waves doing running? —
the grass doing growing?
What is the worm doing
making its hole? —
the sun glowing? — the stone

sitting unmoving. Remove
the stone: A shadow is missing.

The moon is making its circle.
A moth is emerging.
A mountain is shifting. A forest
is burning. A snake
is leaving its skin. A fig tree
is bearing. What am I doing here —
the waves running and hissing?

Dawn is doing its breaking.
The grass is growing.
A buttercup fills with light.
What am I doing? What am I making?
What is the stone doing? Making
its shadow. The worm
is making its hole.

ABOVE THE ARNO

My room in Florence was the color of air.
Blue the stippled wall I woke to,
the tile floor white except where
shadowed by the washstand and my high
bed. Barefoot I'd go to the window to look
at the Arno. I'd open the broad shutters like a book,
and see the same scene. But each day's sky,
or night, dyed it a different light.

The lizard river might be green, or turbid gray,
or yellowish like the stucco palazzi
on the opposite quay.
Boys would be angling with long, lank
poles, sitting on the butts of them, dangling
legs from the paved bank;

they wore handkerchiefs, the corners knotted,
for caps against the strong

sun, and had their dogs along;
the dogs, brown-and-white spotted,
had to lie quiet. But I never saw anything
jerk the lines of the yellow poles.
The boys smoked a lot, and lazed in the sun.
Smaller ones dove and swam in the slow, snaking Arno
right under the sign that read: PERICOLO!
VIETATO DI BAGNARSI.

Over Ponte Trinità, fiacres would go,
or a donkey-driven cart, among the auto
and popping scooter traffic. Freckled, gray,
blinkered horses trotted the red-and-black
carriages in which the richer tourists rode.
(A donkey looks like a bunny under its load,
with its wigwag ears and sweet expression;
the workman-driver flicks

a string-whip like a gadfly over it.)
I'd hear hoof-clops and heel-clicks
among hustling wheels on the bridge, that curved
like a violin's neck across the Arno.
It had two statues at each end —
white, graceful, a little funny.
One, a woman, had lost her head, but strode
forward holding her basket of fruit just the same.

You could see Giotto's Tower in my "book" and
the gold ball on top of Brunelleschi's Dome
and the clock with one hand
on the campanile of the Palazzo Vecchio,
and a blue slice of the Apennines the color of my room.
One day I slept all afternoon —
it was August and very hot — and didn't wake
until late at night,

or rather, early morning.
My mind was fresh — all was silent.
I crossed the white tiles, barefoot,
and opened the book of the shutters
to faint stars, to a full Arno,
starlight fingering the ripples. Gondola-slim
above the bridge, a new moon held a dim
circle of charcoal between its points.

Bats played in the greenish air,
their wing-joints
soft as moths' against the bone-gray palazzi where
not a window was alight,
the doorways dark as sockets.
Each of the four statues so white
and still,
rose somnambulistic from its hill

of stone, above the dusky slide
of the river. On my side,
a muscular, round-polled
man — naked behind — hugged a drape
against him, looking cold.
His partner, fat,
in short toga and hat
made of fruit, leaned a hand on a Horn

of Plenty. On the opposite bank, in torn
sweeping robes, a Signora
bore sheaves of wheat along her arm.
And, striding beside her with stately charm
in her broken flounces, the Headless One*
offered her wealthy basket, chin
up — though I had to imagine
chin, face, head, headdress, all.

* The head of Primavera was later found in October 1961 by workmen in the debris of the
Arno and restored to the statue.

Then a tall
tower began to tell F O U R,
and another with different timbre spelled it
a minute later. Another mentioned it for the third time
in harsh bronze and slow.
Still another, with delicate chime
countered and cantered it. By now the sky had turned
della Robbia blue, the Arno yellowed silver.

I stood between the covers of my book and heard
a donkey's particular heels,
like syllables of a clear, quick word,
echo over the Arno. Then came the scrape-clink
of milk cans lowered on cobbles. And with the moon still
there, but transparent, the sky began to fill
with downy clouds — pink
as the breasts of Botticelli's Venus — foretinting dawn.

MANYONE FLYING

Warm, but stuffy in the middle,
Cold, but clear here on the edge . . .
Out on the ragged edge, flying lonely.
Not all alone, not that brave,
or foolish, or self-sufficient,
or self-believing. In the middle,
between the wingtips of scattered others,
too little space. Too little time . . .
time to think, space to feel
private in, and wonder,
wonder which is Body? *My* body, or the Flock
I fly in — among? Am I a wing
and fly where I decide, Is *It* flying, and I
a feather in the Wing? The others, who hide
in the warm middle, flying, think, I
think, that they are parts. I think too

much, maybe, here   in the clear,
in the chill   spaces. Out on the edge,
my maneuverings,   my wings, think
they are free.   Flock, where do we
fly? Are we Ones?   Or One, only?
If only One, not lonely   . . . being Manyone . . .
but Who   are We? And Why?

THE LIGHTNING

The lightning waked me. It slid unde r
my eyelid. A black book flipped ope n
to an illuminated page. Then insta ntly
shut. Words of destiny were being ut-
tered in the distance. If only I could
make them out! . . . Next day, as I lay
in the sun, a symbol for concei ving the
universe was scratched on my e yeball.
But quickly its point eclipse d, and
softened, in the scabbard of my brain.

My cat speaks one word: Fo ur vowels
and a consonant. He rece ives with the
hairs of his body the wh ispers of the
stars. The kinglet spe aks by flashing
into view a ruby feath er on his head.
He is held by a threa d to the eye of
the sun and cannot fall into error.
Any flower is a per fect ear, or else it
is a thousand lips . . . When will I grope
clear of the entr ails of intellect?

ON THE EDGE

I was thinking, while I was working on my income tax,
here in the open angle of a V —
that blue on the map that's water — my house
tucked into the fold of a hill, on the edge
of a ragged beak of the sea
that widens and narrows according to the tide:
"This little house will be swallowed some year.
Not yet. But threatened."

Chips are houses, twigs are trees
on the woodland ledges along the lip,
the blue throat open, thirsty. Where my chip-roof sits,
sandland loosens, boulders shift downslope,
bared roots of old trunks stumble.
The undermining and undulating lurch
is all one way, the shore dragged south
to spill into and fill another mouth.

I was thinking while I was working: "The April sun
is warm." Suddenly, all the twigs on the privet
budded green, the cardinal flamed and called,
the maple rained its flowerets down
and spread leaf-grown. July's plush roses bloomed,
were blown. A hundred gladioli sunsets in a row
raced to die, and dyed the cove,
while the sea crawled the sand, gnawed on the cliff.

And leisurely, cracks in the flagstones happened,
leaks in the roof. The gateposts crumbled,
mortar in the stone wall loosened,
boards in the porch let the nailheads through.
I was thinking, while April's crocus
poked out of earth on the cesspool top:
"Blueblack winter of water coming — icewhite, rockhard
tide will be pounding the side of the gaping V. . . .

"But smell of the windfresh, salty morning,
flash of the sunwhipped beak of the sea!
Better get last year's layers of old leaves up,
before this year's green bursts out, turns brown,
comes blowing down," I was thinking
while I was working on my income tax.

A SUBJECT OF THE WAVES

Today, while a steamshovel rooted in the cove,
leveling a parking lot for the new nightclub,
and a plane drilled between clean clouds in the October sky,
and the flags on the yachts tied in the basin flipped in the wind,
I watched my footsteps mark the sand by the tideline.
Some hollow horseshoe crab shells scuttled there,
given motion by the waves. I threw a plank back to the waves
that they'd thrown up, a sun-dried, sea-swollen stave
from a broken dinghy, one end square, one pointed, painted green.
Watching its float, my attention snagged and could not get off
the hook of its experience. I had launched a subject
of the waves I could not leave until completed.

Easily it skipped, putting out, prow-end topping every smack
and swell. It kept its surface dry, and looked to float
beyond the jetty head, and so be loose,
exchange the stasis of the beach
for unconceived fluidities and agitations.
It set sail by the luck of its construction.
Lighter than the forceful waves, it surmounted their shove.
Heavier, steadier than the hollows they scooped behind them,
it used their crested threats for coasting free.
Unsplashed by even a drop of spray, it was casual master
of the inconsistent element it rode.

But there was a bias to the moving sea.
The growth and motion of each wave looked arbitrary,

but the total spread (of which each crease was part,
the outward hem lying flat by the wall of sky
at the dim blue other end of the bay's bed)
was being flung, it seemed, by some distant will.
Though devious and shifty in detail, the whole expanse
reiterated constancy and purpose.
So, just as the arrowy end of the plank, on a peak of a wave,
made a confident leap that would clear the final shoal,
a little sideways breaker nudged it enough
to turn it broadside. Then a swifter slap from a stronger comber
brought it back, erasing yards of its piecemeal progress
with one push. Yet the plank turned point to the tide,
and tried again — though not as buoyant, for it had got soaked.
Arrogance undamaged, it conveyed itself again
over obstacle waves, a courageous ski,
not noticing, since turned from shore, that the swells it conquered
slid in at a slant; that while it met them head on,
it was borne closer to shore, and shunted down the coast.

Now a bulge, a series of them, as a pulse quickened in the tide,
without resistance lifted up the plank, flipped it over twice,
and dumped it in the shallows. It scraped on sand.
And so it was put back. Not at the place of its first effort;
a greater disgrace than that: at before the birth
of balance, pride, intention, enterprise.
It changed its goal, and I changed my ambition. Not the open
sea — escape into rough and wild, into unpredictability —
but rescue, return and rest. Release from influence
became my hope for the green painted, broken slat,
once part of a boat.

Its trials to come ashore the cold will of the waves thwarted
more capriciously than its assays into adventure made before.
Each chance it took to dig, with its bent spike,
a grip in the salvage of pebbles and weed and shell
was teasingly, tirelessly outwitted
by dragouts and dousings, slammings and tuggings
of the punishing sea. Until, of its own impulse, the sea

decided to let be,
and lifted and laid, lifted and laid
the plank inert on sand. At tide turn,
such the unalterable compulsion of the sea,
it had to turn its back and rumple its bed
toward the other edge, the farther side of the spread.

I watched my footsteps mark the sand by the tideline.
The steamshovel rooting in the cove had leveled
a parking lot for the new nightclub.
The launch from the yacht basin whooshed around the end
of the pier, toward a sailboat with dropped anchor there,
whose claxon and flipping flag signaled for pickup.
The men with their mallets had finished sinking posts
by the gangplank entrance to the old ferry,
its hold ballasted with cement, painted green and black,
furnished with paneled bar and dining deck.
I watched them hang a varnished sign between the posts,
and letter the name: *The Ark.*
Tomorrow I must come
out again into the sun,
and mark the sand, and find my plank,
for its destiny's not done.

AT TRURO

The sea is unfolding scrolls
and rolling them up again.
It is an ancient diary

the waves are murmuring.
The words are white curls,
great capitals are seen

on the wrinkled swells.
Repeated rhythmically
it seems to me I read

my own biography.
Once I was a sea bird.
With beak a sharp pen,

I drew my signature on air.
There is a chapter when,
a crab, I slowly scratched

my name on a sandy page,
and once, a coral, wrote
a record of my age

on the wall of a water-grotto.
When I was a sea worm
I never saw the sun,

but flowed, a salty germ,
in the bloodstream of the sea.
There I left an alphabet

but it grew dim to me.
Something caught me in its net,
took me from the deep

book of the ocean, weaned me,
put fin and wing to sleep,
made me stand and made me

face the sun's dry eye.
On the shore of intellect
I forgot how to fly

above the wave, below it.
When I touched my foot
to land's thick back,

it stuck like stem or root.
In brightness I lost track
of my underworld

of ultraviolet wisdom.
My fiery head furled
up its cool kingdom

and put night away.
The sea is unfolding scrolls,
and rolling them up.

As if the sun were blind
again I feel the suck
of the sea's dark mind.

OCTOBER

I

A smudge for the horizon
that, on a clear day, shows
the hard edge of hills and
buildings on the other coast.
Anchored boats all head one way:
north, where the wind comes from.
You can see the storm inflating
out of the west. A dark hole
in gray cloud twirls, widens,
while white rips multiply
on the water far out.
Wet tousled yellow leaves,
thick on the slate terrace.

The jay's hoarse cry. He's
stumbling in the air,
too soaked to fly.

2

Knuckles of the rain
on the roof,
chuckles into the drain-
pipe, spatters on
the leaves that litter
the grass. Melancholy
morning, the tide full
in the bay, an overflowing
bowl. At least, no wind,
no roughness in the sky,
its gray face bedraggled
by its tears.

3

Peeling a pear, I remember
my daddy's hand. His thumb
(the one that got nipped by the saw,
lacked a nail) fit into
the cored hollow of the slippery
half his knife skinned so neatly.
Dad would pare the fruit from our
orchard in the fall, while Mother
boiled the jars, prepared for
"putting up." Dad used to darn
our socks when we were small,
and cut our hair and toenails.
Sunday mornings, in pajamas, we'd
take turns in his lap. He'd help
bathe us sometimes. Dad could do
anything. He built our dining table,
chairs, the buffet, the bay window

seat, my little desk of cherry wood
where I wrote my first poems. That
day at the shop, splitting panel
boards on the electric saw (oh, I
can hear the screech of it now,
the whirling blade that sliced
my daddy's thumb), he received the mar
that, long after, in his coffin,
distinguished his skilled hand.

4

I sit with braided fingers
and closed eyes
in a span of late sunlight.
The spokes are closing.
It is fall: warm milk of light,
though from an aging breast.
I do not mean to pray.
The posture for thanks or
supplication is the same
as for weariness or relief.
But I am glad for the luck
of light. Surely it is godly,
that it makes all things
begin, and appear, and become
actual to each other.
Light that's sucked into
the eye, warming the brain
with wires of color.
Light that hatched life
out of the cold egg of earth.

5

Dark wild honey, the lion's
eye color, you brought home
from a country store.

Tastes of the work of shaggy
bees on strong weeds,
their midsummer bloom.
My brain's electric circuit
glows, like the lion's iris
that, concentrated, vibrates
while seeming not to move.
Thick transparent amber
you brought home,
the sweet that burns.

6

"The very hairs of your head
are numbered," said the words
in my head, as the haircutter
snipped and cut, my round head
a newel poked out of the tent
top's slippery sheet, while my
hairs' straight rays rained
down, making pattern on the neat
vacant cosmos of my lap. And
maybe it was those tiny flies,
phantoms of my aging eyes, seen
out of the sides floating (that,
when you turn to find them
full face, always dissolve) but
I saw, I think, minuscule,
marked in clearest ink, Hairs
#9001 and #9002 fall, the cut-off
ends streaking little comets,
till they tumbled to confuse
with all the others in their
fizzled heaps, in canyons of my
lap. And what keeps asking
in my head now that, brushed off
and finished, I'm walking
in the street, is how can those

numbers remain all the way through,
and all along the length of every
hair, and even before each one
is grown, apparently, through
my scalp? For, if the hairs of my
head are numbered, it means
no more and no less of them
have ever, or will ever be.
In my head, now cool and light,
thoughts, phantom white flies,
take a fling: This discovery
can apply to everything.

7

Now and then, a red leaf riding
the slow flow of gray water.
From the bridge, see far into
the woods, now that limbs are bare,
ground thick-littered. See,
along the scarcely gliding stream,
the blanched, diminished, ragged
swamp and woods the sun still
spills into. Stand still, stare
hard into bramble and tangle,
past leaning broken trunks,
sprawled roots exposed. Will
something move? — some vision
come to outline? Yes, there —
deep in — a dark bird hangs
in the thicket, stretches a wing.
Reversing his perch, he says one
"Chuck." His shoulder-patch
that should be red looks gray.
This old redwing has decided to
stay, this year, not join the
strenuous migration. Better here,
in the familiar, to fade.

DIGGING IN THE GARDEN OF AGE
I UNCOVER A LIVE ROOT

(For E.W.)

The smell of wet geraniums. On furry
leaves, transparent drops rounded
as cats' eyes seen sideways.
Smell of the dark earth, and damp
brick of the pots you held, tamped empty.
Flash of the new trowel. Your eyes
green in greenhouse light. Smell of
your cotton smock, of your neck
in the freckled shade of your hair.
A gleam of sweat in your lip's scoop.
Pungent geranium leaves, their wet
smell when our widening pupils met.

THIS MORNING

My glasses are
dirty. The window
is dirty. The binocs
don't focus exactly.
Outside it's about
to snow. Not to mention
my myopia, my migraine
this morning, mist on
the mirror, my age.
Oh, there is the cardinal,
color of apple I used to
eat off my daddy's tree.
Tangy and cocky, he
drops to find
a sunflower seed in

the snow. New snow
is falling on top
of the dirty snow.

SCROPPO'S DOG

In the early morning, past the shut houses,
past the harbor shut in fog, I walk free and
single. It is summer — that's lucky. The whole
day is mine. At the end of our village I stop
to greet Scroppo's dog, whose chain is wrapped
around a large dusty boulder. His black coat
is gray, from crouching every day in the gravel
of Scroppo's yard — a yard by a scrap-filled pond,
where Scroppo deals in wrecked cars and car parts.
I guess he gets them from crashes on the expressway,
or from abandoned junks he loots by the roadside.

I don't know the name of Scroppo's dog. I remember
him, years ago, as a big fierce-looking pup.
It may have been his first day chained there,
or shortly after, that he first greeted me:
his eyes big nuggets shooting orange sparks, his
red tongue rippling out between clean fangs —
fangs as white as lilies of the valley that bloom
in a leafy border by Scroppo's weathered porch.
It was late May, as now, when with sudden joyful
bark, black fur erect and gleaming, the dog
rushed toward me — but was stopped by his chain,
a chain then bright and new. I would have met
and stroked him, but didn't dare get near him,
in his strangled frenzy — in his unbelief —
that something at his throat cut short
his coming, going, leaping, circling, running —
something he couldn't bite through, tripped him:
he could go only so far: to the trash in the weeds

61

at the end of the driveway, to the edge
of the oily, broken cement in back, where Scroppo's
muddy flatbed truck stands at night.

Now, as I walk toward him, the dog growls,
then cowers back. He is old and fat and dirty,
and his eyes spit equal hate and fear.
He knows exactly how far he can strain
from the rock and the wrapped chain. There's
a trench in a circle in the oily dirt his paws
have dug. Days and weeks and months and years
of summer heat and winter cold have been survived
within the radius of that chain.
Scroppo's dog knows me, and wants to come and
touch. At the same time, his duty to expel
the intruder makes him bare his teeth and
bristle. He pounds his matted tail, he snarls
while cringing, alternately stretches toward me
and springs back. His bark, husky and cracked,
follows me for a block, until I turn the corner,
crossing the boundary of the cove.

I've never touched Scroppo's dog, and his
yearning tongue has never licked me. Yet, we
know each other well. Subject to the seasons'
extremes, confined to the limits of our yard,
early fettered by an obscure master in whose
power we bask, bones grow frail while steel
thickens; while rock fattens, passions and
senses pale. Scroppo's dog sniffs dust.
He sleeps a lot. My nose grown blunt, I need
to remember the salty damp of the air's taste
on summer mornings, first snowfall's freshness,
the smoke of burning leaves. Each midday,
when the firehouse whistle blows, a duet
of keen, weird howls is heard, as, at the steep
edge of hopelessness, with muzzle pointed,
ears flat, eyes shut, Scroppo's dog forlornly
yodels in time to the village siren sounding noon.

HORSE

Finally got the horse broke in. It took years.
Now, not strong enough to ride it. It was wild,
and ornery, yes. Which came, in part, from its not
knowing it was a horse, meant to be ridden.
Wouldn't look you in the eye. Shied from looking
itself in the eye. Wouldn't look in the mirror,
especially not in back. Didn't know it *had* a back.
Funny, how it followed. Didn't have to be caught.
It offered its back, asked for the saddle. Or, so
I thought. A joke! Throw you? That
horse wouldn't let you touch lip or nose with your
feeding hand, let alone get a leg over. Yet it hung
around, acting as if. Acting as if. Would come up
behind you, nuzzle your neck. You'd turn, grab
for its mane. It slid away. But never kept
away for long. Unpredictable. Drove you crazy.
Made you ornery. Broke *you*. Wish I was strong now,
and that horse not so strong. It wouldn't take long.
To have it. Gentled. Ready to mount. Eager to have
me. Eating out of its hand.

BLEEDING

Stop bleeding   said the knife.
I would if I   could said the cut.
Stop bleeding   you make me messy with this blood.
I'm sorry   said the cut.
Stop or   I will sink in farther said the knife.
Don't   said the cut.
The   knife did not say it couldn't help it but
it   sank in farther.
If   only you didn't bleed said the knife I wouldn't
have   to do this.
I know   said the cut I bleed too easily I hate
that I   can't help it I wish I were a knife like
you and   didn't have to bleed.
Well   meanwhile stop bleeding will you said the knife.
Yes you   are a mess and sinking in deeper said the cut I
will have   to stop.
Have you   stopped by now said the knife.
I've almost   stopped I think.
Why must you   bleed in the first place said the knife.
For the same   reason maybe that you must do what you
must do said   the cut.
I can't stand   bleeding said the knife and sank in farther.
I hate it too said   the cut I know it isn't you it's
me you're lucky to be   a knife you ought to be glad about that.
Too many cuts around   said the knife they're
messy I don't know how   they stand themselves.
They don't said the cut.
You're bleeding again.
No I've stopped said the cut   see you are coming out now the
blood is drying it will rub   off you'll be shiny again and clean.
If only cuts wouldn't bleed   so much said the knife coming
out a little.
But then knives might become   dull said the cut.
Aren't you still bleeding a   little said the knife.
I hope not said the cut.
I feel you are just a little.
Maybe just a little but I can   stop now.
I feel a little wetness still   said the knife sinking in a
little but then coming out a   little.
Just a little maybe just enough   said the cut.
That's enough now stop now do   you   feel better now said the knife.
I feel I have to bleed to   feel I   think said the cut.
I don't I don't have to   feel said   the knife drying now
becoming shiny.

64

HEARING THE WIND AT NIGHT

I heard the wind coming,
transferred from tree to tree.
I heard the leaves
swish, wishing to be free

to come with the wind, yet wanting to stay
with the boughs like sleeves.
The wind was a green ghost.
Possessed of tearing breath

the body of each tree
whined, a whipping post,
then straightened and resumed
its vegetable oath.

I heard the wind going,
and it went wild.
Somewhere the forest threw itself
into tantrum like a child.

I heard the trees tossing
in punishment or grief,
then sighing, and soughing,
soothing themselves to sleep.

THE FLUFFY STUFF

I want the fluffy stuff to keep coming down.
I'm looking into the garden from the third floor.
I wait for it to settle on brownstone windowsills,
on fire escapes, their narrow iron stairs.
Thin-as-tissue bits fall and rise on spirals of air
like meandering moths, and never reach the ground.

At last, dead vines on the trellis in the sooty
backyard begin to whiten. There sprouts a mat
of white grass. Tips of pickets on the fence
get mittens. Chimney tops in the opposite block
have their hoods and copings furred. The fluffy
stuff catches in crotches of the old ailanthus
whose limbs, like long dark cats stretching
on their backs, expose white bellies.

What began gauzy, lazy, scarce, falls willingly now.
I want it to race straight down, big, heavy, thick,
blind-white flakes rushing down so plentiful, so
opaque and dense that I can't see through the curtains.

WEATHER

I hope they never get a rope on you, weather.
I hope they never put a bit in your mouth.
I hope they never pack your snorts
into an engine or make you wear wheels.

I hope the astronauts will always have to wait
till you get off the prairie
because your kick is lethal,
your temper worse than the megaton.

I hope your harsh mane will grow forever,
and blow where it will,
that your slick hide will always shiver
and flick down your bright sweat.

Reteach us terror, weather,
with your teeth on our ships,
your hoofs on our houses,
your tail swatting our planes down like flies.

Before they make a grenade of our planet
I hope you'll come like a comet,
oh mustang — fire-eyes, upreared belly —
bust the corral and stomp us to death.

YES, THE MYSTERY

Yes, the mystery
the mystery of life
the horrid mystery of it
Many have seen it clearer than I
have sat in it
been stuck in it
stood in it up to their nostrils
and chose not to breathe
rather than suck in its stench
And not breathing is most difficult
To stop to refuse to not-respond
is most difficult
Why even in the abstract
it's enough to make you vomit
Think if those roses
were dipped in tar
Thinking it they are
and your eyelids drop off
your neck will never turn again
and you must stare
at the black leather petals forever
Oh Heavenly Father leave us the illusion
of the flies who cluster the lake of urine
gushed by the horse in the fetid prison
of his stall
and the bliss and energy that spins them
as they bathe and dip their sugar there

THE LITTLE RAPIDS

Over its cliff
splashes the
little rapids,
a braid of glossy
motion in perpetual
flow and toss,
its current rayed
flashing down
crayon veins.

Life-node of my
precipice of bone,
a snake-mouth muscle
spills urgent venom
to soft hills,
to flesh-warm stone.

A replica of all
power's crotched
here in the ribs,
knot and nubbin
of the jutting flood.
Leaps and drops
are instants in
the swirling hour

reiterated from
this hub:

Grief-gusher,
freshet of desire,
snug nest of joy
and fear,
its zest constant
even in sleep,
its padded roar
bounding in the
grotto of the breast.

Hinge of hate and
love, steep springhead,
riddle of my blood,
primal pool of
cruelty, and all
queer sweet thrills . . .
Ravine of my body,
red, incredulous
with autumn,
from here curt death
will hurl me delirious
into the gorge.

DOWNWARD

That there were men.
That we are their ghosts.
That men died long ago.

That there was life.
That ours is merely its shadow.

That we have fallen
from a peak on the high past
and are no longer men.

That this is the reason
for our hopelessness,
the reason our life is crippled.

That we grope
upon the slope of the past
and grasp nothing
but our cravings.

Our forward aims
are but our backward looks.
We can barely remember life
for it belonged to *Them*.

SUBCONSCIOUS SEA

Oh to cast the mind
into that cool green trough
to be washed and dashed
and twirled and dipped
between those waves

Delicious the swipe of a green wave
across this puzzled forehead

And through the span
of a long long night
when the waters are dark
and scarred with silver
oh to drop
this enigmatic clot
down the nebulous stairs of the sea

to rest at last
on the ocean's floor

There beneath layers
of a thousand waves
a thousand veils between it
and the sun
this frail bowl
nuzzled in sand
salt grains sifting its sockets
would come to rest
taste its own eternity

RUSTY AUTUMN

Rusty autumn to your breast again I come   Memorial tears
I leave in tarnished spoons of grass
Hold me Mother though I am grown and you are old
and burning only for death

Sky my childhood   Oh familiar blue cobbled with clouds
and misting now as with a cataract
where has Father gone   the abundant laughter
our tent and shelter   broad shoulders of the sun?
My dad my tall my yellow-bright ladder of delight

Rusty autumn on your flat breast I lie
and rocks and ragweed my ribs feel in the shaggy field
A blemish on each beam of stubble
and its slanting lash of shadow   These are spears
that were your milk-soft breast I trod in the upright green
Summer's flesh lay all the years between
and hid the bloom of hate
seeded that other time the horizontal world heaved
with my tears   Now too late for planting

Oh mummied breast Oh brown Mother hold me
though you are cold   and I am grown   grown old

I WILL LIE DOWN

I will lie down in autumn
let birds be flying

Swept into a hollow
by the wind
I'll wait for dying

I will lie inert unseen
my hair same-colored
with grass and leaves

Gather me
for the autumn fires
with the withered sheaves

I will sleep face down
in the burnt meadow
not hearing the sound of water
over stones

Trail over me cloud
and shadow
Let snow
hide the whiteness of my bones

SECURE

Let us deceive ourselves a little
while   let us pretend that air

is earth   and falling lie resting
within each other's gaze   Let us

deny that flame consumes   that
fruit ripens   that the wave must
break   Let us forget the circle's
fixed beginning marks to the
instant its ordained end   Let us

lean upon the moment and expect
time to enfold us   space sustain
our weight   Let us be still   and
falling lie face to face and drink
each other's breath   Be still
Let us be still   We lie secure

within the careful mind of death

STILL TURNING

Under a round roof the flying
horses, held by their heels to the disk of the
floor, move to spurts from a pillar of
      music, cranked from the past like grainy

      honey. Their ears are wood, their nostrils
painted red, their marble eyes
startled, distended with effort, their
      jaws carved grimaces of

      speed. Round and round go the flying
horses, backs arched in utmost
leaps, necks uptossed or stretched
      out, manes tangled by a wooden

wind. As if lungs of wood inside their
chests pumped, their muscles
heave, and bunch beneath the colored
    traces. Round and round go the flying

    horses. Forked in the saddles are thrilled
children, with polished cheeks and fixed
eyes, who reach out in a stretch of
    ambition, leaning out from the turning

    pillar. They lean out to snatch the
rings, that are all of wood. But there's one of
brass. All feel lucky as, pass after
    pass, they stay fixed to the flying

    horses. The horses' reins and stirrups are
leather. Holes in the rumps spout actual
hair, that hangs to the heels that are held to the
    floor that wobbles around to the reedy

    tune. Their tails sweep out on a little
wind, that stirs the grass around the
disk, where the children sit and feel they
    fly, because real wind flies through their

    hair. There is one motion and it is
round. There is one music, and its
sound issues from the fulcrum that
    repeats the grainy tune, forever

    wound in the flutings of wooden
ears. There is one luck (but it is
rare) that, if you catch, will grant
    release from the circle of the flying

    horses. But round and round on the fixed
horses, fashioned to look as if running
races, the children ride as if made of
    wood, till wrinkles carve their smiling

faces, till blindness marbles all their
eyes. Round and round to the sagging
music, the children, all bewitched by their
     greeds, reach out to gather the wooden

     rings. And each ring makes a finger
stiff, as oil from the fulcrum blackens the
grass. Round and round go the flying
     hearses, carved and colored to look like steeds.

ORDER OF DIET

I

Salt of the soil and liquor of the rock
is all the thick land's food and mead.
And jaws of cattle grip up
stuffs of pasture for their bellies' need.
We, at table with our knives,
cut apart and swallow other lives.

2

The stone is milked to feed the tree;
the log is killed when the flame is hungry.
To arise in the other's body?
Flank of the heifer we glut, we spend
to redden our blood. Then do we send
her vague spirit higher? Does the grain
come to better fortune in our brain?

3

Ashes find their way to green;
the worm is raised into the wing;
the sluggish fish to muscle slides;

eventual chemistry will bring
the lightning bug to the shrewd toad's eye.
It is true no thing of earth can die.

4

What then feeds on us? On our blood
and delectable flesh: the flood
of flower to fossil, coal to snow,
genes of glacier and volcano,
and our diamond souls that are bent
upward? To what Beast's intent
are we His fodder and nourishment?

THE ALYSCAMPS AT ARLES

            The bodies
that covered the bones
                 died.
      Then the bones
                 died.
       Now the stones
that covered the bones
            are dying
                     in the Alyscamps at Arles.

            The lizard darts
            between thick lips
of the hollow–bodied
          stones.
            Under the broken lids
            the scorpion lives
            transfixed.

A sculptor who forms
by destroying form,
and finds form
                    beneath,
has peeled the bodies
and found the bones,
has dwindled the bones
                    till they snapped
                    in the coffin-beds
of the stones.
                    Now he crumbles
                    the heavy limbs
of the stones
that have been dying
                    for two thousand years
                    in the Alyscamps at Arles.

Soft bodies
died
                    soonest.
Flesh
                    was a colored dew wiped off.
Bones
                    were chalk to the sculptor,
                    but he has been rubbing
at these stones
                    for two thousand years.

                    See, they have faces
                    with mouths and sockets.
                    See, in the shadows
                    of the poplars
                    are great square skulls
                    with noseholes dark,
                    like caves.
                    There, where the lizard
                    spreads his saurean hand.

                    Moonlight
        puts a flesh
                    around the recumbent ribs
        of the stones.
                    When the passion
                    of the nightingale begins,
                    the sculptor
                    seems to sleep.

TRINITY CHURCHYARD, SPRING 1961

        Thin shoulders of the old stones.
        Rude weathered signals of the dead.
        Armless and as if wearing square
        robes. Some with an outcrop rounded

        as the head once was. Some dark
        and marred as charcoal, slices broken.
        Torsos rugged earth holds steady here.
        Perpetual in rain and wind and under

        the shrill file of the years.
        Some that were white have yellowed
        in the sun, bent back in a stasis,
        tipped by time. As candles lopped

        or shortened with their use. The names
        have run awry as melted wax.
        Their burning has been opposite to green
        and flame-shaped buds exploding now.

        Gaunt remnants of one great skeleton
        awaiting assembly by the church's side.
        She herself a saintly corpse
        hidden in a corner of the town,

a soot-cowled ornament among the tall,
smooth-sided tombs of glass
whose ostentatious signals on the sky
heedless ask their own erasure.

Their shadows grow and, longer than themselves,
repeat them on their owned and ancient grass.
Among the dead-to-be, that multiply,
huddle the frail dead undestroyed.

NATURE

A large gut, this was the vision.
Mother in hospital, I slept in her bed.
Inside a stomach great as the planet . . .

quagmire ground in gray movement . . .
mucous membrane, rugous, reached my foot
. . . sucked one leg to the crotch . . .

Squirming, sweating, I pulled loose this time.
But it surrounds,
shudders, munches, sucks us down, so

gradually we seldom know.
Until the last sink, where mouth says,
"Here's a Mouth!" Is Nature

this planet only? Or all the universe?
What should we think? Birth
of an infant . . . a film I saw the other day:

Mother-belly, round as the planet,
her navel the North Pole . . .
palpated by rubber fingers . . . Face down,

the wet head, twisting free
of a vomiting Mouth, its mouth
tasting anus as, forced forth, it howled . . .

Muck sealed the squeezed eyes . . .
Mother, eighty-one, fasted five days
and went to Temple. Mormon, her creed

eternal life, she fell
on the kitchen floor unconscious.
The plane flew

over snow-breasts of mountains
no man's track has touched.
June, and blue lilacs in every yard . . .

One bud-nippled bloom I took to her hospital bed.
Her mouth woke to its dew. This time
it woke . . . Last night I slept in her bed.

FEEL ME

"Feel me to do right," our father said on his deathbed.
We did not quite know — in fact, not at all — what he meant.
His last whisper was spent as through a slot in a wall.
He left us a key, but how did it fit? "Feel me
to do right." Did it mean that, though he died, he would be felt
through some aperture, or by some unseen instrument
our dad just then had come to know? So, to do right always,
we need but feel his spirit? Or was it merely his apology
for dying? "Feel that I do right in not trying,
as you insist, to stay on your side. There is the wide
gateway and the splendid tower, and you implore me
to wait here, with the worms!"

Had he defined his terms, and could we discriminate
among his motives, we might have found out how to "do right"

before *we* died — supposing he felt he suddenly knew
what dying was. "You do wrong because you do not feel
as I do now" was maybe the sense. "Feel me, and emulate
my state, for I am becoming less dense — I am feeling right
for the first time." And then the vessel burst,
and we were kneeling around an emptiness.

We cannot feel our father now. His power courses through us,
yes, but *he* — the chest and cheek, the foot and palm,
the mouth of oracle — is calm. And we still seek
his meaning. "Feel me," he said, and emphasized that word.
Should we have heard it as a plea for a caress —
a constant caress, since flesh to flesh was all that we
could do right if we would bless him?
The dying must feel the pressure of that question —
lying flat, turning cold from brow to heel — the hot
cowards there above protesting their love, and saying,
"What can we do? Are you all right?" While the wall opens
and the blue night pours through. "What can we do?
We want to do what's right."

"Lie down with me, and hold me, tight. Touch me. Be
with me. Feel with me. *Feel* me to do right."

DEATH, GREAT SMOOTHENER

Death,
great smoothener,
maker of order,
arrester, unraveler, sifter and changer;
death, great hoarder;
student, stranger, drifter, traveler,
flyer and nester all caught at your border;
death,
great halter;
blackener and frightener,
reducer, dissolver,

seizer and welder of younger with elder,
waker with sleeper,
death, great keeper
of all that must alter;
death,
great heightener,
leaper, evolver,
great smoothener,
great whitener!

LAST DAY

I'm having a sunbath on the rug
alone in a large house facing south.
A tall window admits a golden trough
the length of a coffin in which I lie
in December, the last day of the year.
Sky in the window perfectly empty.
Naked tree limbs without wind.
No sounds reach my ears except their
ringing, and heart's thud hollow and
slow. Uncomplicated peace. Scarcely
a motion. Except a shadow that un-
detected creeps. On the table a clay pot,
a clump of narcissus lengthens its stems.
Blue buds sip the sun. Works of the clock
circle their ratchets. There is nothing
to wish for. Nothing to will.
What if this day is endless? No *new
year* to follow. Alteration done with.
A golden moment frozen, clenched.

THE ENGAGEMENT

When snow   cross
a wing   to where
is folded   I flow
over everything   in the rainbow

when night   seek me
a net   in the rock
dips us   break
in forget   that lock

when blue   meet me
my eye   in the wheel
leaks into   your thread
a sky   I'll feel

and floss   I'll come
your skin   to where you sink
is what the   in the tiger's
spiders spin   blink

when stone   and catch you
our veins   in the fish
are parted   with my strenuous
chains   wish

when prism   Find me
sun   in the flake
bends us   I will
one from one   wake

DAYS

A DAY LIKE ROUSSEAU'S DREAM

Paradise lasts for a day. Crowns of the palms lift
and glisten, their hairy trunks breathe with the sway
of fronds in striped light. Balconies of leaves
mount in layers to lunettes of sky. The ground is
stippled by shadows of birds. In a blink, they flit
into hiding, each disguised against its own color
in the tall leafwall that pockets a thousand nests
and husks, cones, seedpods, berries, blossoms.

Look closely. The whites of creature eyes shift
like diamonds of rain. Flowers are shrieks of color
in the gullies, are shaped to leap or fly, some with
sharp orange beaks or curved purple necks, or they
thrust out vermilion tongues. Velvet clubs, jeweled
whips, silky whisks and puffs and beaded clusters
combine their freakish perfumes.

Beside a slow gray stream, lilies, startling white,
unfurl like crisp breastpocket handkerchiefs.
Hummingbirds upright in flight flash sequined throats.
Eyes of an owl, goldrimmed circles, dilate, then shut
where he stands on a strut in the moiré of a datepalm
umbrella. Smooth trunks of eucalyptus twist up into
sunlight where, on a dangling basketnest, the hooded
oriole swings, ripe apricot.

High on a barkpeeled limb, is that a redhaired gibbon
hanging by one arm? And, drooping from a vine,
a boa's muscular neck, lidless eye and scimitar smile?

Are sagbellied panthers, partly eclipsed in bamboo shade,
gliding behind that thicket? Is there a pygmy,
silver-eyed, black as the cabinet of shadow he hides in,
wearing a cockatoo on top of his ashen frizz?

Paradise lasts for a day. Be seated, with legs akimbo,
central on a mat of moss. Focus and penetrate the long
perspective between the palisades of green. Stabbing
through slits of light, your eyes may find —
couched in fern in a sunny alcove, melonpink body and
blackflagged head, eggshell-eyed, scarlet-lipped —
that magnetic, ample, jungle odalisque.

The eyes of animals enlarge to watch her, as all wind
drains from the leaves, and pure white scuts of cloud
appear in the zenith. Your gaze speeds to target,
the point of the V's black brush, where an oval
crack of space, a pod of white unpainted canvas, splits
for your eye's escape where her thighs do not touch.

SPRING UNCOVERED

Gone the scab of ice that kept it snug,
the lake is naked.

Skins of cloud on torn blue:
sky is thin.

A cruelty, the ribs of trees
ribboned by sun's organdy.

Forsythia's yellow, delicate rags,
flip in the wind.

Wind buckles the face of the lake;
it flinches under a smack of shot.

Robbed of stoic frost, grass
bleeds from gaffs of the wind.

Rock, ridging the lake,
unchapped of its snowcloth, quakes.

But autumn fruits upon the water,
plumage of plum, and grape, and pumpkin bills:

Two mallards ride, are sunny baskets;
they bear ripe light.

And a grackle, fat as burgundy,
gurgles on a limb.

His bottle-glossy feathers
shrug off the wind.

APRIL LIGHT

Lined with light
the twigs are stubby arrows.
A gilded trunk writhes
upward from the roots,
from the pit of the black tentacles.

In the book of spring
a bare-limbed torso
is the first illustration.

Light teaches the tree
to beget leaves,
to embroider itself all over
with green reality,
until summer becomes
its steady portrait,

and birds bring their lifetime
to the boughs.

Then even the corpse
light copies from below
may shimmer, dreaming it feels
the cheeks of blossom.

A CITY GARDEN IN APRIL

The Magnolia

In the shade
each tight cone

untwists to a goblet.
Under light

the rim widens,
splits like silk.
Seven spatulate

white flakes
float open, purple
dregs at the nape.

The Old Ailanthus

Impossible to count
your fingers,

and all of them crooked.
How many tips

intending further tender
tips, in rigid grapple-

clusters weave with the
wind, with the shift

of the puffy rain cloud?
With the first big

honey-heat of the sun
you'll unloose

your secret explosion.
Then impossible to count

all the lubricious torches
in your labyrinth of arms.

Daffodils

Yellow telephones
in a row in the garden
are ringing,
shrill with light.

Old-fashioned spring
brings earliest models out
each April the same,
naïve and classical.

Look into the yolk-
colored mouthpieces
alert with echoes.
Say hello to time.

The Little Fountain

The sun's force
and the fountain's

cool hypnosis —
opposed purities

begin their marathon.
Colorless and motionful

the bowl feels twirl
a liquid hub,

the soft, incessant wheel
slurs over marble

until the dilation frays,
dribbling crystal strings.

The circle encircled,
the reborn circle

synchronized,
repeats the friction,

plash and whisper,
as of feathers rubbed

together or glossy hair.
Bounced from the sun's

breastplate, fierce colors
of flowers, fat leaves,

flinching birds —
while the gray dial

of water keeps all day
its constancy and flicker.

The Vine

You've put out
new nooses since
yesterday.

With a hook and
a hook and a hook
you took territory

over brick,
seized that side
and knitted

outward to snare
the air with knots
and nipples of leaves.

Your old rope-root,
gray and dried,
made us think you'd

died self-strangled.
One day you inflated
a green parachute,

then breezily invented
a tent, and in five
you've proliferated

a whole plumed pavilion.
Not only alive
but splurging

up and out like a geyser.
Old Faithful,
it's worth a winter

hung up stiff
in sullen petrifaction
for such excess.

WATER PICTURE

In the pond in the park
all things are doubled:
Long buildings hang and
wriggle gently. Chimneys
are bent legs bouncing
on clouds below. A flag
wags like a fishhook
down there in the sky.

The arched stone bridge
is an eye, with underlid
in the water. In its lens
dip crinkled heads with hats
that don't fall off. Dogs go by,
barking on their backs.
A baby, taken to feed the
ducks, dangles upside-down,
a pink balloon for a buoy.

Treetops deploy a haze of
cherry bloom for roots,
where birds coast belly-up
in the glass bowl of a hill;
from its bottom a bunch
of peanut-munching children
is suspended by their
sneakers, waveringly.

A swan, with twin necks
forming the figure 3,
steers between two dimpled
towers doubled. Fondly
hissing, she kisses herself,
and all the scene is troubled:
water-windows splinter,
tree-limbs tangle, the bridge
folds like a fan.

A TREE IN SPRING

Now, while that tree just past bud, the leaves
young and small, a pale green haze the morning

sun sifts through; its trunk and limbs, its grasp
of branches, the tendencies of twigs, the whole

shape of its craving like the shoot of a fountain
passionately rising to overflow (but so slow,

so secret it is invisible as motion); the main
limbs from their division low on the trunk

reaching up and out to stab in three directions
(to stab for the light, the light that shifts);

just now, behind its scrim of stippled mist
the solid body of that tree, the whole shape

of its craving is plain to see; while millions
of leaves bud to increase, enlarge and hide

the reaching limbs, the forks and branches, all
the stubby-fingered twigs, thickening quickly

to eclipse remaining slits the morning sun sifts
through; before the leaves' opacity, before

eyelids of the light entirely close, now see,
seize with hasty sight an instant of vision.

IN THE YARD

Dogwood's snow.
Its ground's air.
Redheaded's riddling
the phone pole.
Fat-tailed she-dog
grinning's thrasher-
red. Oriole there
by the feeder's cheddar
under black bold head.
Neighbor doing yard-
work's getting red.
Lifts tiles to
a barrow. L.I.R.R.'s
four cars rollskate by
white potato blooms
farside the field.
That square's our
bedroom window.
You're not there.
You're away, looking
for nails, or such,
to put up a mirror,
frame the Adam and

Eve, bright hair
held back by the
robin's-egg-blue
band. Or you're at
the body shop about
the broken bumper.
Cabbage butterfly's
found honey, he
thinks, on ring glints
on my hand. I wait
for the ringneck,
who trumpets twice,
parades his mate.
She's gray. Comes
the Blue Bug crunching
driveway. You're back,
barefoot, brought
some fruit. Split me
an apple. We'll
get red, white
halves each, our
juice on the
Indian spread.

RAIN AT WILDWOOD

The rain fell like grass growing
upside down in the dark,
at first thin shoots,
short, crisp, far apart,

but, roots in the clouds,
a thick mat grew

quick, loquacious, lachrymose blades
blunt on the tent top.

The grass beneath ticked,
trickled, tickled like rain
all night, inchwormed
under our ears,

its flat liquid tips slipping
east with the slope.
Various tin plates
and cups and a bucket filled

up outside,
played, plinked, plicked,
plopped till guttural.
The raccoon's prowl was almost

silent in the trash,
soggy everything but eggshells.
No owl called.
Waking at first light

the birds were blurred,
notes and dyes of jay and towhee
guaranteed to bleed.
And no bluing in the sky.

In the inverted V
of the tent flaps
muddy sheets of morning
slumped among the trunks,

but the pin oaks' viridian
dripping raggedy leaves
on the wood's floor released
tangy dews and ozones.

CATBIRD IN REDBUD

Catbird in the redbud this morning.
No cat could
mimic that rackety cadenza he's making.
And it's not red,
the trapeze he's swaying on.
After last night's freeze,
redbud's violet-pink, twinkled on
by the sun. That bird's
red, though, under the tail
he wags, up sharply, like a wren.

The uncut lawn hides blue
violets with star-gold eyes on the longest
stems I've ever seen. Going to
empty the garbage, I simply have
to pick some,
reaching to the root of green,
getting my fist dewy, happening
to tear up a dandelion, too.

Lilac, hazy blue —
violet, nods buds over the alley
fence, and (like a horse with a yen
for something fresh for breakfast)
I put my nose into a fragrant
pompom, bite off some, and chew.

SHU SWAMP, SPRING

Young skunk
cabbages all over
the swamp.

Brownish purple,
yellow-specked
short tusks,

they thicken,
twirl and point
like thumbs.

Thumbs of old
gloves, the nails
poked through

and curled.
By Easter, fingers
will have flipped out

fat and green.
Old gloves, brown
underground,

the seams split.
The nails
have been growing.

ONE MORNING IN NEW HAMPSHIRE

We go to gather berries of rain
(sharp to the eye as ripe to the tongue)
that cluster the woods and, low down
between rough-furrowed pine
trunks, melons of sunlight. Morning, young,
carries a harvest in its horn:
colors, shapes, odors, tones
(various as senses are keen).
High in a grape-transparent fan

of boughs are cones
of crystal that were wooden brown.

Two by two, into our ears
are fed sweet pips from a phoebe's throat,
and buzzy notes from a warbler pair,
nuts chuckled from the score
of the thrasher. Gauzing afloat,
a giant moth comes to the choir,
and hums while he sips
from spangles of fern. Insects whir
like wheat in a circular
bin of light; we hear skip
the husking chipmunks in their lair.

Goblin pears, or apples, or quaint
eggs, the mushrooms
litter the forest loft
on pungent mats, in shade still wet,
the gray of gunny in the gloom —
in sun, bright sawdust.
Here's a crop for the nose
(relish to sight as motley to scent):
fume of cobwebbed stumps, musky roots,
resin-tincture, bark-balm, dayspring moss
in stars new-pricked (vivid as soft).

Day heats and mellows. Those winking seeds —
or berries — spill from their pods; the path's dry
from noon wood to meadow. A speckled
butterfly on top of a weed is a red
and yellow bloom: if that two-ply
petal could be touched,
or the violet wing of the mountain!
Both out of reach — too wary,
or too far to stroke, unless with the eye.
But in green silk of the rye
grain our whole bodies are cuddled.

In the sun's heart we are ripe
as fruits ourselves, enjoyed
by lips of wind our burnished slopes.
All round us dark, rapt
bumble-eyes of susans are deployed
as if to suck our honey-hides. Ants nip,
tasting us all over
with tickling pincers. We are a landscape
to daddy-long-legs, whose ovoid
hub on stilts climbs us like a lover,
trying our dazzle, our warm sap.

SKETCH FOR A LANDSCAPE

A clearing her forehead. Brisk wilderness
of hair retreats from the smooth dancing ground,
now savage drums are silent. In caves of shade
twin jaguars couch, flicking their tails
in restless dream. Awake they leap in unison,
asleep they sink like embers.
Sloping swards her cheekbones graduate to
a natural throne. Two lambs her nostrils curled
back-to-back. Follow the shallow hollow to
her lip-points, stung blossoms or bruised fruits,
her lower lip an opulent orchard, her spiral smile
a sweet oasis both hot and cool.
Soft in center, swollen, a bole of moss
hiding white stones and a moist spring
where lives a snake so beautiful and shy,
his undulant hole is kept a slippery secret.
A cleft between the cliff-edge and her mouth,
we drop to the shouldered foothills down the neck's
obelisk, and rest. In the valley's scoop
velvet meadowland.

FLAG OF SUMMER

Sky and sea and sand,
fabric of the day.
The eye compares each band.

Parallels of color on bare
canvas of time-by-the-sea.
Linen-clean the air.

Tan of the burlap
beach scuffed with prints
of bathers. Green and dapple,

the serpentine swipe
of the sea unraveling
a ragged crepe

on the shore. Heavy satin
far out, the coil,
darkening, flattens

to the sky's rim.
There a gauze screen,
saturate-blue, shimmers.

Blue and green and tan,
the fabric changes hues
by brush of light or rain:

sky's violet bar
leans over flinty waves
opaque as the shore's

opaline grains; sea silvers,
clouds fade to platinum,
the sand-mat ripples

with greenish tints
of snakeskin, or drying,
whitens to tent-cloth

spread in the sun. These bands,
primary in their dimensions,
elements, textures, strands:

the flag of summer,
emblem of ease, triple-striped,
each day salutes the swimmer.

HAYMAKING

The sagging hayricks file into the lane
The horses' chests are wading
toward home and evening
Today they gather summer to the barns
The lean-hipped men in aisles of stubble
lurching pitch whole yellow acres
the sun astride their necks all day

Now they rock in tousled cradles
Sweat-dark reins lace idle fingers
Soon to taste evening on the tongue
Evening will smooth their eyelids

By forkfuls they gather summer in
to heap in the cool barns
Snug against the rafters pile the
yellow stuff of summer
Against the crisp walls press
the sweet grasses
Bed down the loft with a shaggy mattress
and line the shady stalls where butterflies
drift through the knotholes

So when winter whistles in the bee
and frets the willow
of her last ragged leaf
when snow leans in the doorsill
at the steaming crib the cow
will munch on summer
With brown bemused stare
pools and pasture shade
juicy banks of green she'll conjure
and absently will wag an ear
at droning memory's fly

SUMMER'S BOUNTY

berries of Straw	nuts of Brazil
berries of Goose	nuts of Monkey
berries of Huckle	nuts of Pecan
berries of Dew	nuts of Grape
berries of Boisen	beans of Lima
berries of Black	beans of French
berries of Rasp	beans of Coffee
berries of Blue	beans of Black
berries of Mul	beans of Jumping
berries of Cran	beans of Jelly
berries of Elder	beans of Green
berries of Haw	beans of Soy
apples of Crab	melons of Water
apples of May	melons of Musk
apples of Pine	cherries of Pie
apples of Love	cherries of Choke
nuts of Pea	glories of Morning
nuts of Wal	rooms of Mush
nuts of Hazel	days of Dog
nuts of Chest	puppies of Hush

HER MANAGEMENT

She does not place, relate, or name
the objects of her hall,
nor bother to repair her ceiling,
sweep her floor, or paint a wall
symmetrical with mountains.

Cylindrical, her tent
is pitched of ocean on one side
and — rakish accident —
forest on the other;
granular, her rug

of many marbles, or of roots,
or needles, or a bog —
outrageous in its pattern.
The furniture is pine
and oak and birch and beech and elm;

the water couch is fine.
Mottled clouds, and lightning rifts,
leaking stars and whole
gushing moons despoil her roof.
Contemptuous of control,

she lets a furnace burn all day,
she lets the winds be wild.
Broken, rotting, shambled things
lie where they like, are piled
on the same tables with her sweets,

her fruits, and scented stuffs.
Her management is beauty.
Of careless silks and roughs,
rumpled rocks, the straightest rain,
blizzards, roses, crows,

April lambs and graveyards,
she *chances* to compose
a rich and sloven manor.
Her prosperous tapestries
are too effusive in design

for our analyses —
we, who through her textures move,
we specks upon her glass,
who try to place, relate, and name
all things within her mass.

FEATHERS

ON ADDY ROAD

A flicker with a broken neck
we found on the road, brought home, and laid
under a beech tree, liver-red the leaves.

On gaming-table green, in autumn shade,
we spread his yellow-shafted wing;
the spokes slid closed when we let go.

Splendid as the king
of spades, black half-moon under chin,
breast of speckled ermine,

scarlet ribbon at the nape —
how long before his raiment fade,
and gold slats tear within the cape?

We left him on the chilly grass.
Through the equinoctial night
we slept and dreamed

of the wetland meadow where,
one tawny dawn, the red fox crept —
an instant only, then his pelt

merged with the windbent reeds,
not to be seen again.
Next morning, going barefoot to the lawn,

we found the flicker's body gone, and saw
in the dew of the sandy road
faint print of a fox's paw.

CAMOUFLEUR

Walked in the swamp   His cheek vermilion
A dazzling prince
Neck-band white   Cape he trailed
Metallic mottled
Over rain-rotted leaves   Wet mud reflected
Waded olive water
His opulent gear   Pillars of the reeds
Parted the strawgold
Brilliance   Made him disappear

ANGELS AT "UNSUBDUED"

All the angels are here this morning, in the striped light
and shade. Some — ruby-eyed, patterned black and tan and white —
are kicking leaves behind them, finding their food.
There are white-throated angels, scarlet-headed angels,
angels of shrill blue. Some bronzed angels are spangling wings
and dabbling iridescent heads in the rain pan.

On cleats down the trunk of a pine descends the downy angel. Her tiny
drill dithers faster than a snare drum. Black-capped or tufted,
round-eyed cherubs flick to ground, scrambling for thrown seed.
The bent-tailed, the brindled, the small red-breasted
next arrive, jab needle-beaks into the suet. Until a cocky
coal-winged angel with red patches elbows them off.

Neat-fronted in clerical gray, cat angels have quietly landed.
They raise their spread tails, flashing rusty coverts.
Rushing on high legs from under the thornbush, an arrogant brown
angel shrieks that he can thrash them all.

Now alights the crimson Pope of angels, masked, with thick
pink nose. He's trailed by two pale female acolytes,
ticking and ruffling crested crowns. Cracking two seeds,

the splendid seraph hops, as if on pogo stick, to each in turn,
to put between accepting beaks the sacrament — they stand agape
for this — an act that's like a kiss.

Yellow-throated angels loop to a wag of honeysuckle, waiting
for a gang of raucous purple angels to finish bathing and fly.
Still kicking leaves under the laurel, shy black-headed, red-eyed,
rufous-sided angels, in light and shadow, stay half hidden.

THE WOODS AT NIGHT

The binocular owl,
fastened to a limb
like a lantern
all night long,

sees where all
the other birds sleep:
towhee under leaves,
titmouse deep

in a twighouse,
sapsucker gripped
to a knothole lip,
redwing in the reeds,

swallow in the willow,
flicker in the oak —
but cannot see poor
whippoorwill

under the hill
in deadbrush nest,
who's awake, too —
with stricken eye

flayed by the moon
her brindled breast
repeats, repeats, repeats its plea
for cruelty.

THE SNOWY

Standing by the wires of your enclosure, I stared into your eyes.
I had to stare until your eyes showed they'd seen me.
You hunched on your cement crag, black talons just showing
beneath your chest. Your beak, like a third gleaming claw, hid
in the white fluff of your face. Your round head, helmet of fleece,
had no neck, no ears. Under your blizzard of feathers your closed
wings were invisible. Elemental form simplified as an egg,
you held perfectly still on your artificial perch. You, too,
might be a crafty fake, stuffed or carved. Except your eyes. Alive,
enormous, yellow circles containing black circles, clear, slick,
heartstopping double barrels of concentrated rage pointed at me.
Without seeing me. Suddenly, your head flicked completely around,
faced straight backwards and swiveled front again.
So quick I doubted you had done it. Then your glass-clear pupils
disappeared, your eyelids of white down slid up over them. Your
face shut. It went blank. Your hooded snow-head looked blind.

I remained beside the wires, leaning toward you, absorbing your
chilling closeness. Constantly shoving past you, the ever-shifting
crowd. Western sunlight slanted into your diorama. Now I saw
your white chest was flecked with dusky. Captivity had soiled you,
had worn and aged you, under the strokes of countless avid eyes.
Eyes such as mine. At feeding time the crowd squabbled to get closer.
Through a slit in the painted wall (a simulation of arctic tundra)
your keeper released a panic of voles and mice. You ignored them,
you let them vanish into crannies of the sculptured rocks.
You settled lower, sullen, on your perch. You gathered emptiness and
silence about you, until you seemed no longer there, no longer alive.

The park had emptied. The gates were closing. I had to leave you.
Perhaps you waited until dark to unhinge your wings, to drift
noiseless down. Perhaps you put hooks into your prey, when they,
grown used to the absence of threat in the air, emerged
with wrinkled noses and scuttled here and there.

FOUNTAIN PIECE

A bird
is perched
upon a wing

The wing
is stone
The bird
is real

A drapery
falls about this form
The form is stone
The dress is rain

The pigeon preens his own
and does not know
he sits upon a wing
The angel does not feel
a relative among her large
feathers stretch
and take his span
in charge
and leave her there
with her cold
wings that cannot fold
while his fan
in air.

The fountain raining
wets the stone
but does not know it dresses
an angel in its tresses

Her stone cheek smiles
and does not care
that real tears
flow there

THE SNOW GEESE AT JAMAICA BAY

A great wedge of snow geese wafted over,
their wings whiter than the white air,
thinned to a long line at one hypotenuse,
as the caravan turned, and pointed north,

a needle their leader, trailing two wavering
threads. Each pair of wings powerful and large,
but in the air, high, weightless as fleece
or petals blown, to lift within the pattern.

Arrowed, yet curved, their course unveering,
varying but carried forward in a ventral glide,
all the star-sharp forms taking their own tilt,
undulant crests on a proud swell, heaving,

hoisting its feather-body toward a divined coast.
And a blue goose flew with them in the dwindling
end of their line. Cooler his color
than the buttermilk breasts of the others,

his dark feet stretched out, his wings
of evening snow. A strange and related other,
denser chip let go, to weight a pure design,
in the wild wedge melted last into the sky.

ONE OF THE STRANGEST

Stuffed pink stocking, the neck,
toe of pointed black, the angled beak,
thick heel with round eye in it upside down, the pate,

swivels, dabbles, skims the soup of pond all day
for small meat. That split polished toe is mouth
of the wading flamingo

whose stilts, the rosy knee joints, bend
the wrong way. When planted
on one straight stem, a big fluffy flower

is body a pink leg, wrung, lifts up over,
lays an awkward shoe to sleep on top of,
between flocculent elbows, the soft peony wings.

PIGEON WOMAN

Slate, or dirty-marble-colored,
or rusty-iron-colored, the pigeons
on the flagstones in front of the
Public Library make a sharp lake

into which the pigeon woman wades
at exactly 1:30. She wears a
plastic pink raincoat with a round
collar (looking like a little

girl) and flat gym shoes,
her hair square-cut, orange.
Wide-apart feet carefully enter
the spinning, crooning waves

(as if she'd just learned how
to walk, each step conscious,
an accomplishment); blue knots in the
calves of her bare legs (uglied marble),

age in angled cords of jaw
and neck, her pimento-colored hair,
hanging in thin tassels, is gray
around a balding crown.

The day-old bread drops down
from her veined hand dipping out
of a paper sack. Choppy, shadowy ripples,
the pigeons strike around her legs.

Sack empty, she squats and seems to rinse
her hands in them — the rainy greens and
oily purples of their necks. Almost
they let her wet her thirsty fingertips —

but drain away in an untouchable tide.
A make-believe trade

she has come to, in her lostness
or illness or age — to treat the motley

city pigeons at 1:30 every day, in all
weathers. It is for them she colors
her own feathers. Ruddy-footed
on the lime-stained paving,

purling to meet her when she comes,
they are a lake of love. Retreating
from her hands as soon as empty,
they are the flints of love.

A PAIR

A he
and she,
prowed upstream,
soot-brown
necks,
bills the green
of spring
asparagus,

heads
proud figure-
heads for the boat-
bodies, smooth
hulls on feathered   the two,
water,   browed with light,
                                  steer ashore,
                                  rise: four
                                        web-
                                  paddles pigeon-
                                          toe it
                                  to the reeds;

                                            he
                                      walks first,
                                      proud, prowed
                                        as when light-
                                      browed, swimming,
                                            he leads.

THE WILLETS

One stood still, looking stupid. The other,
beak open, streaming a thin sound,
held wings out, took sideways steps,
stamping the salt marsh. It looked threatening.
The other still stood wooden, a decoy.

He stamp-danced closer, his wings arose,
their hinges straightened,
from the wedge-wide beak the thin sound
streaming agony-high —
in fear she wouldn't stand? She stood.

Her back to him pretended —
was it welcome, or only dazed
admission of their fate?
Lifting, he streamed a warning
from his beak, and lit

upon her, trod upon her
back, both careful feet.
The wings held off his weight.
His tail pressed down, slipped off. She
animated. And both went back to fishing.

GOODBYE, GOLDENEYE

Rag of black plastic, shred of a kite
caught on the telephone cable above the bay
has twisted in the wind all winter, summer, fall.

Leaves of birch and maple, brown paws of the oak
have all let go but this. Shiny black Mylar
on stem strong as fishline, the busted kite string

whipped around the wire and knotted — how long
will it cling there? Through another spring?
Long barge nudged up channel by a snorting tug,

its blunt front aproned with rot-black tires —
what is being hauled in slime-green drums?
The herring gulls that used to feed their young

on the shore — puffy, wide-beaked babies standing
spraddle-legged and crying — are not here this year.
Instead, steam shovel, bulldozer, cement mixer

rumble over sand, beginning the big new beach house.
There'll be a hotdog stand, flush toilets, trash —
plastic and glass, greasy cartons, crushed beercans,

barrels of garbage for water rats to pick through.
So, goodbye, goldeneye, and grebe and scaup and loon.
Goodbye, morning walks beside the tide tinkling

among clean pebbles, blue mussel shells and snail
shells that look like staring eyeballs. Goodbye,
kingfisher, little green, black-crowned heron,

snowy egret. And, goodbye, oh faithful pair of
swans that used to glide — god and goddess
shapes of purity — over the wide water.

CAMPING IN MADERA CANYON

We put up our tent while the dark closed in
and thickened, the road a black trough
winding the mountain down. Leaving the lantern
ready to light on the stone table,
we took our walk. The sky was a bloom
of sharp-petaled stars.

Walls of the woods, opaque and still,
gave no light or breath or echo, until,
faint and far, a string of small toots —
nine descending notes — the whiskered owl's
signal. A tense pause . . . then, his mate's
identical reply.

At the canyon's foot, we turned,
climbed back to camp, between tall walls
of silent dark. Snugged deep into our sacks,
so only noses felt the mountain chill,
we heard the owls once more. Farther from us,
but closer to each other. The pause, that linked
his motion with her seconding, grew longer
as we drowsed. Then, expectation frayed,
we forgot to listen, slept.

In a tent, first light tickles the skin
like a straw. Still freezing cold out there,
but we in our pouches sense the immense
volcano, sun, about to pour
gold lava over the mountain, upon us.
Wriggling out, we sleepily unhinge,
make scalding coffee, shivering, stand and sip;
tin rims burn our lips.

Daybirds wake, the woods are filling
with their rehearsal flutes and pluckings,
buzzes, scales and trills. Binoculars
dangling from our necks, we walk
down the morning road. Rooms of the woods
stand open. Glittering trunks
rise to a limitless loft of blue. New snow,
a delicate *rebozo*, drapes the peak that,
last night, stooped in heavy shadow.

Night hid this day. What sunrise may it be
the dark to? What wider light ripens to dawn

behind familiar light? As by encircling arms
our backs are warmed by the blessing sun,
all is revealed and brought to feature.
All but the owls. The Apaches believe
them ghosts of ancestors, who build their nests
of light with straws pulled from the sun.

The whiskered owls are here, close by,
in the tops of the pines, invisible and radiant,
as we, blind and numb, awaken — our just-born
eyes and ears, our feet that walk —
as brightness bathes the road.

ABOVE BEAR LAKE

Sky and lake the same blue,
and blue the languid mountain between them.
Cloud fluffs make the scene flow.
Greeny white poles of aspen snake up,
graven with welts and calluses where branches
dried and broke. Other scabs are lover-made:
initials dug within linked hearts and, higher,
some jackknifed peace signs.
A breeze, and the filtered light makes shine
a million bristling quills of spruce and fir
downslope, where slashes of sky and lake
hang blue — windows of intense stain. We take
the rim trail, crushing bloom of sage,
sniffing resinous wind, our boots in the wild,
small, everycolored Rocky Mountain flowers.
Suddenly, a steep drop-off: below we see the whole,
the whale of it — deep, enormous blue —
that widens, while the sky slants back to pale
behind a watercolored mountain.
Western Tanager — we call him "Fireface" —
darts ahead, we climb to our camp

as the sun slips lower. Clipped to the top
of the tallest fir, Olive-sided Flycatcher,
over and over, fierce-whistles, "Whip!
Whip three bears! Whip, whip three bears!"

OCTOBER TEXTURES

The brushy and hairy,
tassely and slippery

willow, phragmite,
cattail, goldenrod.

The fluttery, whistley
water-dimpling divers,

waders, shovelers,
coots and rocking scaup.

Big blue, little green,
horned grebe, godwit,

bufflehead, ruddy,
marsh hawk, clapper rail.

Striated water
and striated feather.

The breast of the sunset.
The phalarope's breast.

WATERBIRD

Part otter, part snake, part bird the bird Anhinga,
jalousie wings, draped open, dry. When slack-
hinged, the wind flips them shut. Her cry,
a slatted clatter, inflates her chin-
pouch; it's like a fish's swim-
bladder. Anhinga's body, otter-
furry, floats, under water-
mosses, neck a snake with white-
rimmed blue round roving eyes. Those long feet stilt-
paddle the only bird of the marsh that flies
submerged. Otter-
quick over bream that hover in water-
shade, she feeds, finds fillets among the water-
weeds. Her beak, ferrule of a folded black
umbrella, with neat thrust impales her prey.
She flaps up to dry on the crooked, look-
dead-limb of the Gumbo Limbo, her tan-
tipped wing fans spread, tail a shut fan dangled.

A NEW PAIR

Like stiff whipped cream in peaks and tufts afloat,
the two on barely gliding waves approach.

One's neck curves back, the whole head to the eyebrows
hides in the wing's whiteness.

The other drifts erect, one dark splayed foot
lifted along a snowy hull.

On thin, transparent platforms of the waves
the pair approach each other, as if without intent.

Do they touch? Does it only seem so to my eyes'
perspective where I stand on shore?

I wish them together, to become one fleece enfolded, proud
vessel of cloud, shape until now unknown.

Tense, I stare and wait, while slow waves carry them
closer. And side does graze creamy side.

One tall neck dips, is laid along the other's back,
at the place where an arm would embrace.

A brief caress. Then both sinuous necks arise,
their paddle feet fall to water. As I stare,
with independent purpose at full sail, they steer apart.

ANOTHER SPRING UNCOVERED

Colors take bodies,
become many birds.
Odors are born
as earliest buds.
Sounds are streams,
the pebbles bells.
Embraces are
the winds and woods.

Hills of lambskin
stroke our feet.
We move in an amnion
of light,
fondle moss
and put our cheeks
to birches
and warm slate

sides of rocks.
Cardinal on a limb
gripped: if we
could take him

into our hand,
the whistling red
feather-pulse,
the velvet plum —

and seize those other
hues, hot, cool:
indigo bunting sky-piece,
olive thrush
in brown shadow,
oriole apricot-breasted,
hush-wing harlequin
towhee — alive!

If we could eat snowdrops,
sip hyacinths,
make butterflies
be bows in our hair,
wade the tinkling streams
of innocence,
wear lambskin grass,
and suck but milk of air!

FEEL LIKE A BIRD

feel like A Bird
understand
he has no hand

instead A Wing
close-lapped
mysterious thing

in sleeveless coat
he halves The Air

skipping there
like water-licked boat

lands on star-toes
finger-beak in
feather-pocket
finds no Coin

in neat head like
seeds in A Quartered
Apple eyes join
sniping at opposites
stereoscope The Scene
Before

close to floor giddy
no arms to fling
A Third Sail
spreads for calm
his tail

hand better
than A Wing?
to gather A Heap
to count
to clasp A Mate?

or leap
lone-free and mount
on muffled shoulders
to span A Fate?

STRIPPING AND PUTTING ON

I always felt like a bird blown through the world.
I never felt like a tree.

I never wanted a patch of this earth to stand in,
that would stick to me.

I wanted to move by whatever throb my muscles
sent to me.

I never cared for cars, that crawled on land or
air or sea.

If I rode, I'd rather another animal: horse, camel,
or shrewd donkey.

Never needed a nest, unless for the night, or when
winter overtook me.

Never wanted an extra skin between mine and the sun,
for vanity or modesty.

Would rather not have parents, had no yen for a child,
and never felt brotherly.

But I'd borrow or lend love of friend. Let friend be
not stronger or weaker than me.

Never hankered for Heaven, or shied from a Hell,
or played with the puppets Devil and Deity.

I never felt proud as one of the crowd under
the flag of a country.

Or felt that my genes were worth more or less than beans,
by accident of ancestry.

Never wished to buy or sell. I would just as well
not touch money.

Never wanted to own a thing that I wasn't born with.
Or to act by a fact not discovered by me.

I always felt like a bird blown through the world.
But I would like to lay

the egg of a world in a nest of calm beyond
this world's storm and decay.

I would like to own such wings as light speeds on,
far from this globule of night and day.

I would like to be able to put on, like clothes,
the bodies of all those

creatures and things hatched under the wings
of that world.

MAKINGS

THE PLAYHOUSE

Here is the playhouse of weather-faded white
Trees like legs of elephants stamp round it
in the mossy light after rain
It sits on a knoll   Its chimney is red
Troll-headed weeds press against the pane

A rabbit could hop the tidy picket fence
but the gate is locked beneath the little wicket
Stooping you can peer like a marionette master
into a room with a table and chair   a sofa in the corner
with antimacassar   a hearth a scuttle and broom

The child is at the table bent above her game
The fire stretches in the grate
With doll-round eyes intent and oranged by the flame
she plays a little black machine
with clever buttons that she taps

spelling out her name perhaps   And now the plaything
is a square of cloth upon a rack   the child a boy
in one hand a plate where colored knobs are stuck
in the other something like a wand
with which he gambles   It's a game of luck

or magic   Like a stage the playhouse
or like a fairy book improbable and charming
Each time you look inside you see a different play
Is that a toy piano he's diddling on today?
Odd how they never see you watching

Now she's making up a dance
He's buffeting a lump of mud into a fancied shape
Out in the giant wood birds with beaks agape
listen   In gauzy trance the deer stand still
They sense there's something queer

Is the playhouse really here you wonder
and what's it to do with you?
There's a spatter of rain   there's thunder
In a flick of lightning will you see what it means
or will it disappear?

Are the children real if the forest is?
On the path that leads to the playhouse on its knoll
next time you come will there be a hole
matted with weeds?   What if it's you who's missing
or at least invisible   too large a beast for the landscape?

Your feet do not impress the moss
or make a sound among the plodding trees
impassive in the rain   Turn round
Can you see the playhouse?   No it's gone
Now do you feel the loss and the puzzling pain?

DEAR ELIZABETH*

Yes, I'd like a pair of *Bicos de Lacre* —
meaning beaks of "lacquer" or "sealing wax"?
(the words are the same in Portuguese)
". . . about 3 inches long including the tail,
red bills and narrow bright red masks . . ."
You say the male has a sort of "drooping
mandarin-mustache — one black stripe" —

otherwise the sexes are alike. "Tiny but
plump, shading from brown and gray on top
to pale beige, white, and a rose red spot
on the belly" — their feathers, you tell
me, incredibly beautiful "alternating
lights and darks like nearly invisible
wave-marks on a sandflat at low tide,

and with a pattern so fine one must put on
reading glasses to appreciate it properly."
Well, do they sing? If so, I expect their
note is extreme. Not something one hears,
but must watch the cat's ears to detect.
And their nest, that's "smaller than a fist,
with a doorway in the side just wide enough

for each to get into to sleep." They must
be very delicate, not easy to keep. Still,
on the back porch on Perry St., here, I'd
build them a little Brazil. I'd save every
shred and splinter of New York sunshine
and work through the winter to weave them
a bed. A double, exactly their size,

with a roof like the Ark. I'd make sure to
leave an entrance in the side. I'd set it

* A reply to Elizabeth Bishop in Brazil.

in among the morning-glories where the
gold-headed flies, small as needles' eyes,
are plentiful. Although "their egg is apt
to be barely as big as a baked bean . . ."
It rarely hatches in captivity, you mean —

but we could hope! In today's letter you
write, "The *Bicos de Lacre* are adorable as
ever — so tiny, neat, and taking baths
constantly in this heat, in about ¼ inch
of water — then returning to their *filthy*
little nest to lay another egg — which
never hatches." But here it might! And it

doesn't matter that "their voice is weak,
they have no song." I can see them as I
write — on their perch on my porch. "From
the front they look like a pair of half-
ripe strawberries" — except for that stripe.
"At night the cage looks empty" just as
you say. I have "a moment's fright" —

then see the straw nest moving softly.
Yes, dear Elizabeth, if you would be so
kind, I'd like a pair of *Bicos de Lacre* —
especially as in your P.S. you confess,
"I already have two unwed female wild
canaries, for which I must find husbands
in order to have a little song around here."

IN THE BODIES OF WORDS

For Elizabeth Bishop (1911–1979)

Tips of the reeds silver in sunlight. A cold wind
sways them, it hisses through quills of the pines.
Sky is clearest blue because so cold. Birds drop down
in the dappled yard: white breast of nuthatch, slate
catbird, cardinal the color of blood.

Until today in Delaware, Elizabeth, I didn't know
you died in Boston a week ago. How can it be
you went from the world without my knowing?
Your body turned to ash before I knew. Why was there
no tremor of the ground or air? No lightning flick
between our nerves? How can I believe? How grieve?

I walk the shore. Scraped hard as a floor by wind.
Screams of terns. Smash of heavy waves. Wind rips
the corners of my eyes. Salty streams freeze on my face.
A life is little as a dropped feather. Or split shell
tossed ashore, lost under sand. . . . But vision lives!
Vision, potent, regenerative, lives in bodies of words.
Your vision lives, Elizabeth, your words
from lip to lip perpetuated.

Two days have passed. Enough time, I think, for death
to be over. As if your death were not *before* my knowing.
For a moment I jump back to when all was well and ordinary.
Today I could phone to Boston, say Hello. . . . Oh, no!
Time's tape runs forward only. There is no replay.

Light hurts. Yet the sky is dull today. I walk the shore.
I meet a red retriever, young, eager, galloping
out of the surf. At first I do not notice his impairment.
His right hind leg is missing. Omens. . . .
I thought I saw a rabbit in the yard this morning.
It was a squirrel, its tail torn off. Distortions. . . .

Ocean is gray again today, old and creased aluminum
without sheen. Nothing to see on that expanse.
Except, far out, low over sluggish waves, a long
clotted black string of cormorants trails south.
Fog-gray rags of foam swell in scallops up the beach,
their outlines traced by a troupe of pipers —
your pipers, Elizabeth! — their racing legs like spokes
of tiny wire wheels.

Faintly the flying string can still be seen.
It swerves, lowers, touching the farthest tips of waves.
Now it veers, appears to shorten, points straight out.
It slips behind the horizon. Vanished.

But vision lives, Elizabeth. Your vision multiplies,
is magnified in the bodies of words.
Not vanished, your vision lives from eye to eye,
your words from lip to lip perpetuated.

Bethany, Delaware
October 13–15, 1979

SPRING *BY ROBERT LOWELL*
(PHOTOGRAPH BY TRUDI FULLER)

. . . only an ear is in the spring.

Sunlight in Central Park it could
be:yond his shoulders the bench back
a field for play: that's over
exposed as video: fuzzy. Or is it Boston
Common: maybe May be:hind him?
Well: well light's be:hind him. Gray
shades his face: is it a tree
trunk's toppled roots' dark riot he sees
casts shadow on him: be:fore him? Only

an ear and flesh of part
of a neck in sunlight: some
of the right side of his shirt. A wish
bone drawing pinches brows:
parenthe-seizes lips: the eyes
dim be:cause of shadow: not him:
fright light white tight
pellets in pupils: absent in photo

flash his gaze that must be:spectacled.
Be:fore head shows a setting
sun reflected: light's spot on wavelet
thought not sinking yet. A warm
ear's drinking infant
light. Be:side him's morning in the spring
Park: a hot beam rubbing the right
side of his dark coat: baring
as if a gray breast there.

PICASSO: "DREAM." OIL. 1932

She dreams a landscape. On her chest
a moon from breathing waves rises,
the nipple of her breast.

She dreams the left side of her face.
Grown from her chin — in profile, green —
a penis purples up to place

the oval of her cheek. She dreams her eye
closed in the wrinkle of its head.
She dreams its root: red smile.

NAKED IN BORNEO

(From a painting by Tobias)

They wear air
or water like a skin,
their skin the smoothest suit.
Are tight and loose
as the leopard, or sudden
and still as the moccasin.
Their blouse is black

shadows of fronds
on a copper vest of sun.
Glossy rapids are
their teeth and eyes
beneath straight harsh blonds
of rained-on grain that thatch
their round head-huts.

Long thongs their bodies, bows
or canoes. Both tense and lax

their bodies, spears
they tool, caress, hoard, decorate
with cuts. Their fears
are their weapons. Coiled or
straight they run up trees

and on jungle thorns; their feet
are their shoes, fiercehair
their hats that hold off sun's hate.
They glide, muscles of water
through water, dark oil-beads
pave their lashing
torsos. Are bare in air,

are wind-combed, armpit and groin;
are taut arrows turned sinuous reeds
for dancing on drumskin ground.
Rasped by the sun's tongue, then moon-licked
all their slick
moist feathered shafts
in the hammocks of tangled thighs

the silks of night plash among.
Their joys, their toys are their children
who as kittens ride
their mother's neck, or wrestle
with the twins of her breasts
where she squats by the meal pot.
At hunter's naked side

little hunter stalks fix-eyed,
miniature poison-dart
lifted, learning the game:
young pointer in the bush,
fish-diver in the river,
grave apprentice in the art
of magic pain

when the blood pines
to be let a little,
to sharpen the friction of Alive,
in the feckless skin
leave some slits and signs
that old spirit leaked out,
new spirit sneaked in.

MY FARM

The page my acre; A, B, C are buildings.

Blue is the name of the barn
already in place by the meadow.

Name! Name! shout the hammers.
The house rides up in three strokes —
its attic tri-cornered like art,
its porch the shape of ample.

Blue is the hump of the barn.
Call the cows: Come, Black. Come, White.

On Cadmium, the center field,
a structure I haven't guessed is going to be guyed.
A kind of planetarium?
Ask the architect in the morning.

This is my property.
I erase it if I please.

Or plant a skating pond.

The problem is to build a floor like that,
that moves their legs like that, like scythes.

All the page is a white pond now.

Some boys have fallen, and gotten up:
those red streaks are their cheeks and ears.

A man with silver hair advances —
and a woman on one blade;
she holds a muff of huge sunlight.

The whole sheet, solid, runs beneath between their feet.
I pull it smooth and backwards
until, far up, it rumples among the trees.

Today — let's see — I'll trade weathers.
Hoist a hall of sagebrush.
Or the stairs of a waterfall.

Have the high rooms hung with clouds.
The only furniture some horses.

The brown divans graze on the rugs.

THE RED BIRD TAPESTRY

Now I put on the thimble of dream
    to stitch among leaves the red node of his body
and fasten here the few beads of his song.

Of the tree a cage of gilded spines
    to palace his scarlet, cathedral his cry,
and a ripple from his beak I sew,
    a banner bearing seven studs,
this scarf to be the morning that received his stain.

I do with thought instead of actuality
    for it has flown.

With glinting thimble I pull back, pull back
   that freak of scarlet to his throne:

To worship him, enchanted cherry to a tree
   that never bore such fruit —
who tore the veil of possibility
   and swung here for a day,
a never-colored bird, a never-music heard,
   who, doubly wanded then, looped away.

To find, in hollow of my throat, his call,
   and try his note on all the flutes of memory,
until that clear jet rinses me
   that was his single play —
for this I wear his daring and his royal eye.

Now perfected, arrested in absence —
   my needle laid by and spread my hand —
his claws on stems of my fingers fastened,
   rooted my feet and green my brow,
I drink from his beak the seven beads dropping:
   I am the cage that flatters him now.

DREAM AFTER NANOOK

Lived savage and simple, where teeth were tools.

Killed the caught fish, cracked his back in my jaws.
Harpooned the heavy seal, ate his steaming liver raw.
Wore walrus skin for boots and trousers. Made knives
   of tusks. Carved the cow-seal out of her hide
   with the horn of her husband.

Lived with huskies, thick-furred as they.
Snarled with them over the same meat.
Paddled a kayak of skin, scooted sitting over the water.

Drove a skein of dogs over wide flats of snow.
Tore through the tearing wind with my whip.

Built a hive of snow-cubes cut from the white ground.
Set a square of ice for window in the top.
Slid belly-down through the humped doorhole.
Slept naked in skins by the oily thighs
    of wife and pup-curled children.

Rose when the ice-block lightened, tugged the chewed boots on.

Lived in a world of fur — fur ground — jags of ivory.
Lived blizzard-surrounded as a husky's ruff.
Left game-traps under the glass teeth of ice.
Snared slick fish. Tasted their icy blood.
Made a sled with runners of leather.

Made a hat from the armpit of a bear.

GOODNIGHT

He and the wind   Harsh as a dog's tongue
She and the house   the licking wind
                                upon her throat

Slow from the house   Rough it wraps
whose mellow walls   and fondles her
have fondled him   as slow into the night
slow from the   he walks
yellow threshold
to the purple wind   She and the house now only
                                He and the wind

INSTINCTS

NEWS FROM THE CABIN

1

Hairy was here.
He hung on a sumac seed pod.
Part of his double tail hugged the crimson
    scrotum under cockscomb leaves —
    or call it blushing lobster claw, that swatch —
    a toothy match to Hairy's red skullpatch.
Cried *peek!* Beaked it — chiseled the drupe.
His nostril I saw, slit in a slate whistle.
White-black dominoes clicked in his wings.
Bunched beneath the dangle he heckled with holes,
    bellysack soft, eye a brad, a red-flecked
    mallet his ball-peen head, his neck its haft.

2

Scurry was here.
He sat up like a six-inch bear,
    rocked on the porch with me;
    brought his own chair, his chow-haired tail.
Ate a cherry I threw.
Furry paunch, birchbark-snowy, pinecone-brown back,
    a jacket with sleeves to the digits.
Sat put, pert, neat, in his suit and his seat, for a minute,
    a frown between snub ears, bulb-eyed head
    toward me sideways, chewed.
Rocked, squeaked. Stored the stone in his cheek.
Finished, fell to all fours, a little roan couch;
    flurried paws loped him off, prone-bodied,
    tail turned torch, sail, scarf.

147

Then, Slicker was here.
Dipped down, cobalt and turquoise brushes
    fresh as paint. Gripped a pine-tassle,
    folded his flaunts, parted his pointed nib, and scrawled
    jeeah! on the air.
Japanned so smooth, his head-peak and all his shaft:
    harsh taunts from that dovey shape, soft tints —
    nape and chin black-splintered, quilltips white-lashed.
Javelin-bird, he slurred his color,
    left his ink-bold word here; flashed off.
Morning prints his corvine noise elsewhere,
    while that green toss still quivers with his equipoise.

4

And Supple was here.
Lives nearby at the stump.
Trickled out from under, when the sun struck there.
Mud-and-silver-licked, his length — a single spastic muscle —
    slid over stones and twigs to a snuggle of roots, and hid.
I followed that elastic: loose
    unicolored knot, a noose he made as if unconscious.
Until my shadow touched him: half his curd
    shuddered, the rest lay chill.
I stirred: the ribbon raised a loop;
    its end stretched, then cringed like an udder;
    a bifid tongue, his only rapid, whirred
    in the vent; vertical pupils lit his hood.
That part, a groping finger, hinged, stayed upright.
Indicated what? That I stood
    in his light? I left the spot.

ALTERNATE HOSTS

I

Am I sitting on your wrist, someone immense?
Are you watching me with tolerant surprise
as I gobble up a gnat, as I slowly draw him
between the double bulges of my face?
His head first, then his body, his wings a garment
whose limp rags have no taste — but his jellied grit
clicks — can you hear it? — mashed against my palate.

My forelegs are placed like elbows on a table.
My needle-narrow rump with its down-bent end
pulses as I munch; it is transparent;
soon you'll see my dinner swim down there.

My biplane wings hold sunlight in their struts;
the whole spectrum plays there on my "harp"
a complete arpeggio of holy color, but
the undersides, you note, have a bitten look
where old battles with the air have frayed them.

I munch and grind. He's halfway in at last.
A pleasure, you think, this eating? It's hard work,
as anyone's business is, and I am thorough.
When I get this one down I have to cruise for more.

2

You are sitting on me somewhere, something wee.
On me, or in me, I don't know which.
And with your sort of prayer you make an itch,
but I can't tell where. Is it in my blood?
Your world, vast, a single corpuscle to me;
to you an unmapped galaxy my smallest muscle.

I'm aware of what you're doing there. Your throat is working
to disgorge what comes out backwards. It's a thought,
black-bodied between awkward wings, and torn
by your palate's struggle when your speech was born.
Bumbling, fuzzy, belligerent, inept, you draw one breath,
while it draws two, before both it and you
are blown away by death.

Never mind, go do your duty, be diligent. Spit out
your poem, your prayer, your quaint explosion. If enough
of you get together there on the same project,
at the root of something, somewhere, sometime,
you might make one hair of me stand on end.
Then you'll see my finger come to smear
the batch of you with one scratch.

A COUPLE

A bee rolls in the yellow rose.
Does she invite his hairy rub?
He scrubs himself in her creamy folds.
A bullet soft imposes her spiral
and, spinning, burrows
to her dewy shadows.
The gold grooves almost match
the yellow bowl.
Does his touch please or scratch?
When he's done his honey-thieving
at her matrix, whirs free, leaving,
she closes, still tall, chill,
unrumpled on her stem.

FABLE FOR WHEN THERE'S NO WAY OUT

Grown too big for his skin,
and it grown hard,

without a sea and atmosphere —
he's drunk it all up —

his strength's inside him now,
but there's no room to stretch.

He pecks at the top
but his beak's too soft;

though instinct or ambition shoves,
he can't get through.

Barely old enough to bleed
and already bruised!

In a case this tough
what's the use

if you break your head
instead of the lid?

Despair tempts him
to just go limp:

Maybe the cell's
already a tomb,

and beginning end
in this round room.

Still, stupidly he pecks
and pecks, as if from under

his own skull —
yet makes no crack . . .

No crack until
he finally cracks,

and kicks and stomps.
What a thrill

and shock to feel
his little gaff poke

through the floor!
A way he hadn't known or meant.

Rage works if reason won't.
When locked up, bear down.

ZAMBESI AND RANEE

Because their mothers refused to nurse them, the two female animals in this compartment were reared together by hand from early infancy. . . . They are firm friends and strongly resent separation. While Zambesi, the lion, is inclined to be rough and aggressive, Ranee, the tiger, easily dominates her.

     —from a plaque at the Bronx Zoo

The tiger looks the younger and more male,
her body ribbed with staves as black as Bengal's
  in the next den. Clear green her eyes,
  in the great three-cornered head, set slantwise;
her hips as lean, her back as straight,
she's a velvet table when she walks, and able
  to bound ten feet to the level where her meat
  is flung at feeding time.

The lion, square-bodied, heavy-pelted, less grand,
her maneless, round-eared head held low,
    slouches and rocks in sand-colored nakedness,
    drag-bellied, watchful and slow; her yellow eyes
jealous, something morose in the down-hook
    of her jaw; her tail, balled at the end,
    like a riding crop taps at the bars.

They twine their shared pavilion, each spine
tracing an opposite figure eight. Paired females,
    they avoid each other's touch; but if, passing,
    as much as a whisker of that black-and-orange head
grazes the lion's flank, her topaz eye narrows:
    irascibly she turns with slugger's paw
    to rake the ear of her mate.

Then rampant, they wrestle; rich snarls
in coils pour from their throats and nostrils.
    Like soft boulders the bodies tumble each other down.
    And then, not bothering to rise, they lounge,
entangled chest to chest. Not hate embroils them,
but that neither will be humble to the other;
    nor will the tiger, in earnest, test her quickness
    against the lion's weight.

Few sights can still surprise us in the zoo,
    though this is the place for marvels.
These odd heroines do attract us. Why?
Crouched on sinewy elbows, sphinxes, they project
    vast boredom. Those still heads outstare
    some horizon of catlike time, while we, in vain,
expect a gleam from eye to eye between them,
a posture of affection, or some clue . . .

Bemused at the bars, some watchers smile and read
Zambesi and Ranee upon their card:
    They might ring the bell, introduce themselves
    and be welcome. The life these ladies lead,
upon a stage, repeats itself behind the walls

of many city streets; silent, or aloud,
the knowing crowd snickers.

Refused to nurse them, simpering mothers read,
and tighten the hold on Darling's hand: "Look
   at the pussy cats!" they coax, they croon,
   but blushing outrage appalls their cheeks —
that this menage calls down no curse,
not only is excused, but celebrated.
   They'd prefer these captives punished, who
   appear to wear the brand some captivated humans do.

BRONCO BUSTING, EVENT #1

The stall so tight he can't raise heels or knees
when the cowboy, coccyx to bareback, touches down

tender as a deerfly, forks him, gripping the rope-
handle over the withers, testing the cinch,

as if hired to lift a cumbersome piece of brown
luggage, while assistants perched on the rails arrange

the kicker, a foam-rubber band around the narrowest,
most ticklish part of the loins, leaning full weight

on neck and rump to keep him throttled, this horse,
"Firecracker," jacked out of the box through the sprung

gate, in the same second raked both sides of the belly
by ratchets on booted heels, bursts into five-way

motion: bucks, pitches, swivels, humps, and twists,
an all-over-body-sneeze that must repeat

until the flapping bony lump attached to his spine is gone.
A horn squawks. Up from the dust gets a buster named Tucson.

MOTHERHOOD

She sat on a shelf,
her breasts two bellies
on her poked-out belly,
on which the navel looked
like a sucked-in mouth —
her knees bent and apart,
her long left arm raised,
with the large hand knuckled
to a bar in the ceiling —
her right hand clamping
the skinny infant to her chest —
its round, pale, new,
soft muzzle hunting
in the brown hair for a nipple,
its splayed, tiny hand picking
at her naked, dirty ear.
Twisting its little neck,
with tortured, ecstatic eyes
the size of lentils, it looked
into her severe, close-set,
solemn eyes, that beneath bald
eyelids glared — dull lights
in sockets of leather.

She twitched some chin-hairs,
with pain or pleasure,
as the baby-mouth found and
yanked at her nipple;
its pink-nailed, jointless
fingers, wandering her face,
tangled in the tufts
of her cliffy brows.
She brought her big
hand down from the bar
with pretended exasperation
unfastened the little hand,
and locked it within her palm —

while her right hand
with snag-nailed forefinger
and short, sharp thumb, raked
the new orange hair
of the infant's skinny flank —
and found a louse,
which she lipped, and
thoughtfully crisped
between broad teeth.
She wrinkled appreciative
nostrils which, without a nose,
stood open — damp holes
above the poke of her mouth.

She licked her lips, flicked
her leather eyelids —
then, suddenly flung
up both arms and grabbed
the bars overhead.
The baby's scrabbly fingers
instantly caught the hair —
as if there were metal rings there —
in her long, stretched armpits.
And, as she stately swung,
and then proudly, more swiftly
slung herself from corner
to corner of her cell —
arms longer than her round
body, short knees bent —
her little wild-haired,
poke-mouthed infant hung,
like some sort of trophy,
or decoration, or shaggy medal —
shaped like herself — but new,
clean, soft and shining
on her chest.

WEDNESDAY AT THE WALDORF

Two white whales have been installed at
the Waldorf. They are tumbling slowly
above the tables, butting the chandeliers,
submerging, and taking soft bites
out of the red-vested waiters in the
Peacock Room. They are poking *fleur-de-lys*
tails into the long pockets on the
waiters' thighs. They are stealing
breakfast strawberries from two eccentric
guests — one, skunk-cabbage green with
dark peepers — the other, wild rose and
milkweed, barelegged, in Lafayette loafers.
When the two guests enter the elevator,
the whales ascend, bouncing, through all
the ceilings, to the sixth floor. They
get between the sheets. There they turn
candy-pink, with sky-colored eyes, and
silver bubbles start to rise from velvet
navels on the tops of their heads.
Later, a pale blue VW, running on poetry,
weaves down Park Avenue, past yellow
sprouts of forsythia, which, due to dog-do
and dew, are doing nicely. The two
white whales have the blue car in tow
on a swaying chain of bubbles. They are
rising toward the heliport on the Pan Am
roof. There they go, dirigible and slow,
hide-swiping each other, lily tails flipping,
their square velvet snouts stitched with
snug smiles. It is April. "There's
a kind of hush all over the world."

BISON CROSSING NEAR MT. RUSHMORE

There is our herd of cars stopped,
staring respectfully at the line of bison crossing.
One big-fronted bull nudges his cow into a run.
She and her calf are first to cross.
In swift dignity the dark-coated caravan sweeps through
the gap our cars leave in the two-way stall
on the road to the Presidents.
The polygamous bulls guarding their families from the rear,
the honey-brown calves trotting head-to-hip
by their mothers — who are lean and muscled as bulls,
with chin tassels and curved horns —
all leap the road like a river, and run.
The strong and somber remnant of western freedom
disappears into the rough grass of the draw,
around the point of the mountain.
The bison, orderly, disciplined by the prophet-faced,
heavy-headed fathers, threading the pass
of our awestruck stationwagons, Airstreams and trailers,
if in dread of us give no sign,
go where their leaders twine them, over the prairie.
And we keep to our line,
staring, stirring, revving idling motors, moving
each behind the other, herdlike, where the highway leads.

DEATH INVITED

Death invited to break his horns
on the spread
cloth. To drop his head
on the dragged flag on the sand.
Death's hoofs slipping
in blood, and a band
of blood down the black side.
Death's tongue, curved in the open mouth

like a gray horn, dripping
blood. And
six colored agonies decking the summit
of his muscled pride.
Death invited to die.

The head
of death, with bewildered raging eye,
flagged down,
dragged down to the red
cloth on the sand.
Death invited to stand,
legs spread,
on the spot of the cape.
To buckle stubborn knees and lie
down in blood on the silken shape.
Beg blindness come to the sun-pierced eye.

The sword, sunk at the top of the shoulder's pride —
its hilt a silver cross — drawn forth now lets
hot radiant blood slide
from bubbling nostrils
through cloth to thirsty ground.

Yearning horns found
fleeing cloth and bloodless pillow,
substance none. Arrogant thighs,
that swiped and turned death by,
now, close as love, above lean lunging,
filling the pain-hot eye.

That stares till it turns to blood.
With the short knife dug
quick!
to the nape.
And the thick
neck drops on the spot of the cape.

Chains are drawn
round the horns, whose points are clean.
Trumpets shout.
New sand is thrown
where death's blood streamed.
Four stout,
jingling horses with gilded hoofs
tug death out.

Life is awarded ears and flowers.
Pelted with hats and shoes, and praise,
glittering life, in tight pink thighs,
swaggers around a rotunda of screams and *Olés*.

Death is dragged from the ring,
a clumsy hide,
a finished thing —
back to his pen.
The gate swings shut.

The gate swings wide.
Here comes trotting, snorting death
let loose again.

BIG-HIPPED NATURE

Big-hipped nature bursts forth the head of god
from jungle clots of green
from pelvic heave of mountains
On swollen-breasted clouds he fattens and feeds
He is rocked in the crib of the sea

Stairways of the inner earth he crawls
and coos to us from the caves
The secret worms miracle his veins
Myriads of fish embellish his iridescent bowels

In multiple syllables the birds
inscribe on air his fledgling words

Swift and winding beasts with coats of flame
serpents in their languor black and blind
in the night of his dark mind express
his awe and anger his terror and magicness

Wherever we look his eye lies bottomless
fringed by fields and woods
and tragic moons
magnify his pupils with their tears

In fire he strides
Within the waterfall
he twines his limbs of light
Clothed in the wind and tall
he walks the roofs and towers
Rocks are all his faces
flowers the flesh of his flanks
His hair is tossed with the grasses everywhere
Stained by the rainbow every shell
roars his whispered spell

When sleep the enormous shadow of his hand descends
our tongues uncoil a prayer
to hush our ticking hearts our sparrow-like fear
and we lie naked within his lair
His cabalistic lightnings play upon us there

EACH LIKE A LEAF

Each like a leaf
like a wave
To be replaced repeated

What do we crave
heated by cerebral
fire?

Transitive as flames
that turn
in a furnace

Or sleet falling
separately settling
to one sheet

Forms faced alike
we dance in some
frame

We are a sea its waves
cannot name
only be

We are a thick wood
by its leaves made
not understood

As flames
their flight and snow
its white

do not perceive
We weave asleep
a body

We awake unravel
the same veins
we travel

ALL THAT TIME

I saw two trees embracing.
One leaned on the other
as if to throw her down.
But she was the upright one.
Since their twin youth, maybe she
had been pulling him toward her
all that time,

and finally almost uprooted him.
He was the thin, dry, insecure one,
the most wind-warped, you could see.
And where their tops tangled
it looked like he was crying
on her shoulder.
On the other hand, maybe he

had been trying to weaken her,
break her, or at least
make her bend
over backwards for him
just a little bit.
And all that time
she was standing up to him

the best she could.
She was the most stubborn,
the straightest one, that's a fact.
But he had been willing
to change himself —
even if it was for the worse —
all that time.

At the top they looked like one
tree, where they were embracing.
It was plain they'd be
always together.

Too late now to part.
When the wind blew, you could hear
them rubbing on each other.

OUT OF THE SEA, EARLY

A bloody
egg yolk. A burnt hole
spreading in a sheet. An en-
raged rose threatening to bloom.
A furnace hatchway opening, roaring.
A globular bladder filling with immense
juice. I start to scream. A red hydrocepha-
lic head is born, teetering on the stump of
its neck. When it separates, it leaks rasp-
berry from the horizon down the wide esca-
lator. The cold blue boiling waves cannot
scour out that band, that broadens, slid-
ing toward me up the wet sand slope. The
fox-hair grows, grows thicker on the
upfloating head. By six o'clock,
diffused to ordinary gold,
it exposes each silk thread and rumple in the carpet.

GODS | CHILDREN

They are born naked,
and without tails.
They cannot fly.
Their blood is red.
They are children until they die,
and then "are God's children."
Are gods . . . children . . .
Are *gods children*?

Worlds are their heads,
oceans infants' serene eyes.
Blue and green they invented.
Leaves did not grow
or the wind blow
until their spine
lifted like a tendril.
Their tongue curled.
Their hand made a sign.

They are not like fruit
though their skin is sweet.
Though they rot they have wrought
the numbers one to ten.
They founded the sun.
When the sun found them
it undertook its path and aim.
The moon, also,
when it received its name.
The air first heard itself called glory
in their lungs.

Beasts they placed in the sky
and in their caves
and on their platforms,
for they remembered their cradles,
their blood in flow
told them their beginnings.
The beloved hoofs,
massy necks,
rich nostrils,
sex, a red coal in the groin,
they worshipped.
Also their helical rod
called evil and sapience.

They ensorcelled angels,
dreamed queerer forms,

on the brain's map fixed a junction, "Infinity,"
in the entrail's maze, "Prophecy,"
and made "Measure"
and the dance of "The Particles,"
with a switch the system, "Time," turned on,
a braided chain,
torque for the whole of space
their game.

They play,
are flexible jugglers and jongleurs,
fashioners of masks;
are mirror-makers
and so dupe themselves,
dress themselves,
are terrified at flesh,
think each other phantoms,
idols, demons, toys;
make of each other handles, ladders, quicksands;
are to each other houses of safety,
hammocks of delight.

They cannot fly,
but nest themselves in bullets
and, dressed as embryos,
shoot out to a circle beyond their ball.
And can breathe with such a placenta,
their foot floating
far separate from its ground.

Before, in iron capsules
lived under the sea,
in baskets inflated rode the air.
Many other marvels built besides.
Are mysterious charts
beneath their skulls' membranes.
And have invented madness.

Under their bodies' casings
in intricate factories
work their strong, soft engines.
Their blood is red.
Color and name they invented,
and so created it.
And have named themselves.

And it is even so
that they operate upon one another,
and increase,
and make replicas,
and replace one another,
new for old,
and tick to death
like moments.

When they are dead,
they are made naked,
are washed and dressed.
They do this for each other
like children.
And are fixed into fine boxes
like children fix their dolls.

And then?
"Are God's children."
Are gods . . . children . . .
Then are gods children?

THE PROCESS

Lie down upon your side
  and fold your knees
    Bend your hands at the wrist
   against your chest
    as a cat or dog does in repose

   Close your eyes and feel
    your brow smooth out like a small
    cloth in the wind
    or a brook slipping
     to gentle waterfall

    Now wait for what will happen
    Something will

     Beneath this hill of breathing hair
    a steep mine
     Within this ear
      oracles of echoes seep
       Wide and clear the eyelid's dome
      a galaxy where suns collide
       and planets spin and moons begin

      Words are birds perceived
      in a secret forest
       Fed by nerve and vein they hop
       from twig to twig and up
        an ivory ladder to the top
         where it is light and they remain
        and are believed

HEAVENS

ONCE THERE WERE GLACIERS

Earth, not flat, not round, your skin loose as a dog's:
earthquakes your hackles raised. When swollen within,
panting you spin, wobbling at the poles. Your hide,
shifting, splits apart, the oceans leak and spread between.
Volcanoes hemorrhage from your gut. Earth, your ruptures,
glaciers, typhoons, arid Saharas — catastrophies, agonies —
are these the process and necessity, throes of eternal
labor? Earth, will you ever be born?

SLEEPING OVERNIGHT ON THE SHORE

Earth turns
            one cheek to the sun
while the other tips
            its crags and dimples into shadow.
We say sun comes up,
            goes down,
but it is our planet's incline
            on its shy invisible neck.
The smooth skin of the sea,
            the bearded buttes of the land
blush orange,
            we say it is day.
Then earth in its turning
            slips half of itself away
from the ever burning.
            Night's frown

smirches earth's face,
              by those hours marked older.
It is dark, we say.
              But night is a fiction
hollowed at the back of our ball,
              when from its obverse side
a cone of self-thrown shade
              evades the shining,
and black and gray
              the cinema of dreams streams through
our sandgrain skulls
              lit by our moon's outlining.

Intermittent moon
              that we say climbs
or sets, circles only.
              Earth flicks it past its shoulder.
It tugs at the teats of the sea.
              And sky
is neither high
              nor is earth low.
There is no dark
              but distance
between stars.
              No dawn,
for it is always day
              on Gas Mountain, on the sun —
and horizon's edge
              the frame of our eye.

Cool sand on which we lie
              and watch the gray waves
clasp, unclasp
              a restless froth of light,
silver saliva of the sucking moon —
              whose sun is earth
who's moon to the sun —
              To think this shore,

each lit grain plain
        in the foot-shaped concaves
heeled with shadow,
        is pock or pocket
on an aging pin
        that juggler sun once threw,
made twirl among
        those other blazing objects out
around its crown.
        And from that single toss
the Nine still tumble —
        swung in a carousel of staring light,
where each rides ringleted
        by its pebble-moons —
white lumps of light
        that are never to alight,
for there is no down.

THE DAY MOON

The day moon, a half ball of snow vaulting
the mountain, was thrown last night by the level east
from a heavy fist.

Its chunk, of metal, passed the pole among the pelting
stars, one curve sliced, the other cupped
in the upright dark, of charcoal. Looped

the parabola of west, lost weight and glamour,
a plaster socket, kneecap-shaped, or as if hammer-
dented. Porous, marrow-old, dawn tossed

it lower. Shrank in the pink net of the sun, a shell
so light no pitch could give it force. Fell
on cold and solid morning, an almost-ball

rolled by a hard hand. Halts
so, until the day aloft the mountain melts,
softens it, bitten wafer, slips it down.

THE CLOUD-MOBILE

Above my face is a map.
Continents form and fade.
Blue countries, made
on a white sea, are erased,
and white countries traced
on a blue sea.

It is a map that moves:
faster than real,
but so slow.
Only my watching proves
that island has being,
or that bay.

It is a model of time.
Mountains are wearing away,
coasts cracking,
the ocean spills over,
then new hills
heap into view
with river-cuts of blue
between them.

It is a map of change.
This is the way things are
with a stone or a star.
This is the way things go,
hard or soft,
swift or slow.

CUMULI

Is it St. Peter's or St. Paul's this dome
reminds you of?
This blue enameled basin upside down
is it of London Luxembourg or Rome?

Would Blake know how to call it pure
yet grand
Would Shakespeare standing where I stand
compare these clouds to Michelangelo?

I have never traveled never seen
those treasure piles of history hewn
to the golden mean
art more ravishing than nature
fabled yield
gemmed sediment of centuries

This Western field under the summer noon
with sibilant lucerne sown
columned with poplars is my Parthenon
On immense blue
around its vaulted walls
alabaster shapes inhabit beauty's pedestals

FLYING HOME FROM UTAH

Forests are branches of a tree lying down,
its blurred trunk in the north.
Farms are fitted pieces of a floor,

tan and green tiles that get smoother,
smaller, the higher we fly.
Heel-shaped dents of water I know are deep

from here appear opaque, of bluish glass.
Curl after curl, rivers are coarse locks
unraveling southward over the land;

hills, rubbed felt, crumpled bumps
of antlers pricking from young bucks' heads.
Now towns are scratches here and there

on a wide, brown-bristled hide.
Long roads rayed out from the sores of cities
begin to fester and crawl with light —

above them the plane is a passing insect
that eyes down there remark, forget
in the moment it specks the overcast.

It climbs higher. Clouds become ground.
Pillows of snow meet, weld into ice.
Alone on a moonlit stainless rink

glides the ghost of a larva, the shadow
of our plane. Lights go on
in the worm-belly where we sit;

it becomes the world, and seems to cease
to travel — only vibrates, stretched out tense
in the tank of night.

The room of my mind replaces the long, lit room.
I dream I point my eye over a leaf
and fascinate my gaze upon its veins:

A sprawled leaf, many-fingered, its radial
ridges limber, green — but curled,
tattered, pocked, the brown palm

nibbled by insects, nestled in by worms:
One leaf of a tree that's one tree of a forest,
that's the branch of the vein of a leaf

of a tree. Perpetual worlds
within, upon, above the world, the world
a leaf within a wilderness of worlds.

LANDING ON THE MOON

When in the mask of night there shone that cut,
we were riddled. A probe reached down
and stroked some nerve in us,
as if the glint from a wizard's eye, of silver,
slanted out of the mask of the unknown —
pit of riddles, the scratch-marked sky.

When, albino bowl on cloth of jet,
it spilled its virile rays,
our eyes enlarged, our blood reared with the waves.
We craved its secret, but unreachable
it held away from us, chilly and frail.
Distance kept it magnate. Enigma made it white.

When we learned to read it with our rod,
reflected light revealed
a lead mirror, a bruised shield
seamed with scars and shadow-soiled.
A half-faced sycophant, its glitter borrowed,
rode around our throne.

On the moon there shines earth light
as moonlight shines upon the earth . . .
If on its obsidian we set our weightless foot,
and sniff no wind, and lick no rain
and feel no gauze between us and the Fire,
will we trot its grassless skull, sick for the homelike shade?

Naked to the earth-beam we will be,
who have arrived to map an apparition,
who walk upon the forehead of a myth.

Can flesh rub with symbol? If our ball
be iron, and not light, our earliest wish
eclipses. Dare we land upon a dream?

ORBITER 5 SHOWS HOW EARTH LOOKS FROM THE MOON

There's a woman in the earth, sitting on
her heels. You see her from the back, in three-
quarter profile. She has a flowing pigtail. She's
holding something
in her right hand — some holy jug. Her left arm is thinner,
in a gesture like a dancer. She's the Indian Ocean. Asia is
light swirling up out of her vessel. Her pigtail points to Europe
and her dancer's arm is the Suez Canal. She is a woman
in a square kimono,
bare feet tucked beneath the tip of Africa. Her tail of long hair is
the Arabian Peninsula.   A woman in the earth.

A man in the moon.

Note: A telephoto of the earth, taken from above the moon by Lunar Orbiter 5 (printed in the *New York Times* August 14, 1967), appeared to show the shadow-image of "a woman in a square Kimono" between the shapes of the continents. The title is the headline over the photo.

AFTER THE FLIGHT OF RANGER 7

Moon, old fossil,
to be scrubbed

and studied like
a turtle's stomach,

prodded over
on your back,

invulnerable hump
that stumped us,

pincers prepare to
pick your secrets,

bludgeons of light
to force your seams.

Old fossil, glistening
in the continuous rain

of meteorites
blown to you from

between the stars,
stilt feet mobilize

to alight upon you,
ticking feelers

determine your fissures,
to impact a pest

of electric eggs
in the cracks

of your cold
volcanoes. Tycho,

Copernicus, Kepler,
look for geysers,

strange abrasions,
zodiacal wounds.

OF ROUNDS

MOON
      round
           goes around while going around a
                          round
                            EARTH.
EARTH
      round
           with MOON
                  round
                  going around while going around,
goes around while going around a
                  round
                  SUN.
SUN
    round
        with EARTH
             round
                with MOON
                      round
                        going around while going
around, and MERCURY
            round
              and VENUS
                round
                  going around while

going around, and MARS

                       round

                             with two MOONS

                                             round

                                           round

                                               going around

while going around, and JUPITER

                              round

                                    with fifteen MOONS

                                               round

round

round

round

round

round

round

round

round

round

round

round

round

round

round

going around while going around, and SATURN

                                 round

                                    with fifteen

MOONS

    round

    round

    round

    round

    round

    round

    round

    round

    round

    round

round
round
round
round
round

     going around while going around, and URANUS

          round

with five MOONS

    round
    round
    round
    round
    round

     going around while going around, and NEPTUNE

round

  with two MOONS

      round
      round

      going around while going around, and

PLUTO

  round

    going around while going around, goes around while

going around

    A

     OF ROUNDS

         Round

COMET WATCH ON INDIAN KEY—
NIGHT OF APRIL 10, 1986

Bright splendid head of
Halley's Comet . . . Comet
coming. Coming again.
Not seen since May 8, 1910.
Called Dirty Snowball, and
Finger of God Pointing,

and Plunger to Disaster . . .
Dis-aster means bad star.
Comet coming. Coming again,
elliptically swishing out
from behind the far
blind side of Sun. Gaseous
Dustball, probably lumpy,
it lets nest, in its
diaphanous tail thinned by
the Solar Wind, Aldebaran
and Betelgeuse undimmed.
Comet coming coming again.
Wonder of wonders . . . Who
will be on watch on that
spring night in 2062?

SEEING JUPITER

A chair was placed
upon the lawn.
In cloak of wind
and shadow, I
sat and bent
my eye upon
a rim of dark
that glittered up
to open heaven.
In the cup
a worn dime,
size of an iris
of anyone's eye:
flat, cold, lost,
found coin
of enormous time.
Some small change
around it: three
little bits swirled,

or else my ragged eye
with wind swung.
In a black
pocket, behind
that blank, hung
hidden a fourth
moon dot; smarting
beneath my tongue,
dreg of ancient mint;
my retina tasted
light how long
dead? My hair
thrashed. Enlarged
upon the lawn,
my chair
I sat in, that wind
and shadow bent,
had slid an inch
toward dawn.

THE SOLAR CORONA *

Looks like a large
pizza with too much
tomato sauce (the fiery

islands in the melted
cheese, the jagged rim,
red bulge of crust)

served on a square
black tray, a "spectro
heliographic diagram

of the sun in the extreme
ultraviolet region of
the spectrum." This

pizza is 400 times
larger than the moon.
Don't burn your lips! —

the deep red regions
are coolest, the white
(ricotta) hottest.

* Cover picture on *Scientific American*, October 1973

AS LONG AGO AS FAR AWAY

"Look there," the star man says. Before our eye
he fixes a funnel of mirrors, a trap for light.
"Out there, that chink — really a chunk — at the top
of the dome, is long ago as it is far away.
Whether it *is*, we do not know. We know it *was*.
We draw, by a thread of light, through this elongate maze
a star long dead, its actual ghost."

"So here the past is caught?" we ask the star man.
"Caught up to us? Is this how time is space,
how miles are years? You've brought *then* down to *now*.
Where shall we look to find the third side of the triad?
From this seat, here at the junction of past and
present, will we peer out someday, to see the future
meet, and so triangulate a Room?"

"Another scope, with prisms ground from clear materials,
must be found," says the star man. "We used to look up,"
we say. "Now we look out. Look out for what has been!
What's past is gathering back to us. Well, then, where's *when* —
the coming to be?" "Still down, and in — in the brain's pen,"
says the star man. "There are the mirrors made to catch,
at birth, the next earth," says the star man.

SKOPUS

The eye
deals with
space. What organ
feels time? Open to our
face, perhaps the
wheels of Long Ago and To Take
Place are turning. Nothing
conceals them. But to
trace them, new
eels of perception must
race from our brow. When a star
keels from the
vase of the sky,
reels of the fishing pupils
pace it to the brain.
Mobiles of duration and passage may
interlace a "distance" where
unpeels an embryo (its
grimace already forming "nearby") whose
steles can caliper and
encase light, easy as our eye
seals planets up up there. "Sometime" may
erase those
creels to catch light in our head — a total
carapace clapped on may "blind" us so that inward space
reveals time's stalled vehicle, the universe at rest upon its
base.

SURVEY OF THE WHOLE

World's lopsided
                That's its trouble
Don't run in a circle
                Runs in a loop
Too much winter
                In the wrong place
Too much summer
                Around the sun
World's gimpy
                Been turning so long
It's lumpy
                A bad top
Day's not long enough
                Spins on a nail
Night's too long
                Bent out of kilter.
World's a lemon
                Wobbles in a loop
Around the sun
                It's not an orange
Won't ever be sweet
                Turns too fast
Turns too slow
                Can't ripen
Too much desert
                Too much snow

VISIONS

LOOK CLOSER

The petals and leaves look much alike, in shape,
texture, rib-pattern, and size. Alike in all but
color. Clusters of red petals intensify the green
of leaves afloat around their stems. Red as
rooster comb at winter's peak, by spring the blooms
appear to be turning green, just as the leaves
are showing streaks of scarlet.

Look closer. By April, at the hub of each wheel
of petals a green knob swells, erects a hairlike
stem with infant leaf attached. It's pale green.
Meanwhile, some older, larger leaves have reddened.
As flimsy petals shrink, young leaves of like size
high on the stems turn red. Or were they petals
that transposed to green? It seems that leaves
and flowers crave to impersonate each other.

Look closer. Nothing so symmetrical takes place.
Toward summer the red clusters, that were showiest
at Christmas, look less bold. The transvestite
behavior of this plant is plain and can be traced.
When young, some leaves do imitate soft petals,
even assume their silks. Especially those born
close to the blooms. Lower, on spindles of stems,
broad leaves with serrate lobes stay frankly distinct
from oval petals. It's at the growing tip,
where leaves touch cheeks with flowers, that they
later begin to blush.

Look closer. By the time some spokes of bloom
have thinned, young, smooth, adjacent leaves have
halfway reddened. Too easy to think that petals
turn leaf-green while leaves go petal-red. Reds
do *not* turn green — not one, not ever. And not *all*
greens go red. Just those born late, at the crown.

By midsummer, if anything is left of this audacious
plant, the petals having thinned, dried, and dropped,
it will look ordinary, not a bit ambiguous.
There'll be an assemblage of leaves with various
lobes sharp-pointed, recalling the shapes of stubby
Christmas trees. And all green?

Look closer. See that the few broad, lowest leaves,
now coarse, curled and ready to fall, show dark
bruise-reds of autumn.

A NAVAJO BLANKET

Eye-dazzlers the Indians weave. Three colors
are paths that pull you in, and pin you
to the maze. Brightness makes your eyes jump,
surveying the geometric field. Alight, and enter
any of the gates — of Blue, of Red, of Black.
Be calmed and hooded, a hawk brought down,
glad to fasten to the forearm of a Chief.

You can sleep at the center,
attended by Sun that never fades, by Moon
that cools. Then, slipping free of zigzag and
hypnotic diamond, find your way out
by the spirit trail, a faint Green thread that
secretly crosses the border, where your mind
is rinsed and returned to you like a white cup.

BY MORNING

Some for everyone
   plenty

  and more coming

Fresh   dainty   airily arriving
   everywhere at once

Transparent at first
   each faint slice
   slow   soundlessly tumbling

   then quickly thickly a gracious fleece
   will spread like youth   like wheat
   over the city

Each building will be   a hill
   all sharps made round

   dark worn noisy narrows made still
   wide   flat   clean   spaces

Streets will be   fields
   cars be   fumbling sheep

A deep bright harvest will be seeded
   in a night

By morning we'll be   children
   feeding on manna

   a new loaf on every doorsill

THE NORTH RIM

Great dark bodies, the mountains.
Between them wriggling the canyon road,
little car, bug-eyed, beaming, goes
past ticking and snicking of August insects,
smell of sage and cedar, to a summit of stars.
Sky glints like fluorescent rock.
Cloth igloo erected, we huff up our bed,
listen to the quaking of leaf-hearts
that, myriad, shadow our sleep.

At dawn, the bodies discovered rugged, oblate,
Indian-warpaint-red, a rooster crows.
Barefoot in brickdust, we strike our tent.
Car crawls the knee of the Great White Throne.
Chiseled by giant tomahawks, the slabs.
In half-finished doorways broad gods stand.
Wind-whipped from the niches, white-throated swifts
razor the void.
We rise to ponderosa, to deer park, to moraine,
mountain bluebirds stippling the meadows,
and coast to the Grand Rim:

Angular eels of light
scribble among the buttes and crinoline
escarpments. Thunder's organ tumbles
into the stairwell of the gorge.
When rain and mist divide their veil,
westering sun, a palette knife, shoves into the cut
colors thick and bright, enclabbering
every serrate slant and vertical;
hard edged, they jut forward,
behind, beside them purple groins and pits
in shadow. Shadow within shadow beneath a shawl
of shadow darkens, and we dare not blink
till light tweaks out.

Morning at Cape Royal. A Merry-Go-Round
out there in the red cirque, Brahma's Temple.
Many Pavilions make a Great
                              Pavilion.
                    Where mountain
              peaks eroded to flat
         ranges, flat ranges broke
         and parted, became pediments,
     and pointed pediments, pinnacles, were
         honed to skinny minarets,
or else, inverted cones, big-headed totems —
Look: On the slope a stone Boot two miles high,
the hip-end slouched in folds, some seven-leaguer
left six million years.
A lizard where I sit, with petrific eye,
is Dinosaur's little cousin
watching me from Juniper's bony root.

Two coils of the river seen from here,
muddy infinite oozing heavy paint.
Each object has its shadow. Or, if not,
must vanish. Now while the sun leans,
tabernacles form. Allow dark openings,
violet-cool arcades. Establish bases,
though colosseums, carved by the shift
of a cloud, descend pendant,
and Great sinks into shadow.
We must go. It rains. The car trickles east
over the frogback of the Kaibab Forest.
I must imagine morning, from Angel's Window
how to dive, firebrushed by the sun.

SPEED

Winnipeg to Medicine Hat, Manitoba, Canada

In 200 miles
a tender painting
on the wind-

shield, not yet done,
in greeny yellows,
crystalline pinks,

a few smeared
browns. Fuselages
split on impact,

stuck, their juices
instantly dried. Spat-
tered flat out-

lines, superfine
strokes, tokens of
themselves flying,

frail engines
died in various
designs: mainly arrow-

shapes, wings gone,
bellies smitten
open, glaze and tincture

the wipers can't
erase. In 400 miles
a palette, thick

impasto; in 600
a palimpsest the sun
bakes through. Stained

glass, not yet done
smiting the wind-
borne, speeds on.

THE GARDEN AT ST. JOHN'S

Behind the wall of St. John's in the city
in the shade of the garden the Rector's wife
walks with her baby a girl and the first
its mouth at her neck seeking and sucking
in one hand holding its buttocks its skull
cupped by the other her arms like a basket
of tenderest fruit and thinks as she fondles
the nape of the infant its sweat is like dew

like dew and its hair is as soft as soft
as down as the down in the wingpits of angels

The little white dog with the harlequin eye
his tail like a thumb feet nimble as casters
　　　scoots in the paths of the garden's meander
behind the wall of St. John's in the city
　　　a toy deposed from his place in her arms
by this doll of the porcelain bone
　　　this pale living fruit without stone

She walks where the wrinkling tinkling fountain
　　　laps at the granite head of a monk
where dip the slippery noses of goldfish
　　　and tadpoles flip from his cuspid mouth
A miracle surely the young wife thinks
　　　from such a hard husband a tender child
and thinks of his black sleeves on the hymnbook
　　　inside the wall of St. John's in the city
the Ah of his stiff mouth intoning Amen
　　　while the organ prolongs its harmonious snore

Two trees like swans' necks twine in the garden
　　　beside the wall of St. John's in the city
Brooding and cool in the shade of the garden
　　　the scrolled beds of ivy glitter like vipers

A miracle surely this child and this garden
　　　of succulent green in the broil of the city
she thinks as setting the bird-cries apart
　　　she hears from beneath the dark spirals of ivy
under the wall of St. John's in the city
　　　the rectal rush and belch of the subway
roiling the corrugate bowels of the city
　　　and sees in the sky the surgical gleam
of an airplane stitching its way to the West
　　　above the wall of St. John's in the city
ripping its way through the denim air

THE SURFACE

First I saw the surface,
then I saw it flow,
then I saw the underneath.

In gradual light below
I saw a kind of room,
the ceiling was a veil,

a shape swam there
slow, opaque and pale.
I saw enter by a shifting corridor

other blunt bodies
that sank toward the floor.
I tried to follow deeper

with my avid eye.
Something changed the focus:
I saw the sky,

a glass between inverted trees.
Then I saw my face.
I looked until a cloud

flowed over that place.
Now I saw the surface
broad to its rim,

here gleaming, there opaque
far out, flat and dim.
Then I saw it was an Eye:

I saw the Wink that slid
from underneath the surface
before it closed its lid.

ON HANDLING SOME SMALL SHELLS
FROM THE WINDWARD ISLANDS

Their scrape and clink
together of musical coin.

> Than the tinkling of crickets
> more eerie, more thin.

Their click, as of crystal,
wood, carapace and bone.

> A tintinnabular fusion.
> Their friction spinal and chill

as of ivory embryo
fragments of horn

> honed to whistles and flutes.
> Windy Eustachian coils

cold as the sea till held,
then warm as the palm,

> and snuggled naturally there
> smoother than skin.

The curve and continuous
spiral intrinsic, their

> role eternal inversion,
> the closed, undulant scroll.

Even when corrugate,
sharpness rubbed from

> their forms, licked by
> the mouth of the sea

to tactile charms.
Some blanched by the eye

        of the sun, a pumice shine
        buffing their calcareous

nakedness clean as a tooth.
Some colored like flesh,

        but more subtle than
        corpuscle dyes. Some

sunsets, some buttermilk
skies, or penumbras

        of moons in eclipse.
        Malachite greens, fish-eyed

icy blues, pigeon-foot pinks,
brindled fulvous browns,

        but most white like tektites.
        Gathered here in a bowl,

their ineradicable inks
vivid, declarative

        under water. Peculiar fossil-
        fruits that suck through ribbed

lips and gaping sutures
into secret clefts

        the sweet wet with a tame taste.
        Vulviform creatures, or

rather, their rocklike
backs with labial bellies.

Some earhole shaped, or
funnels with an overlap,

some stony worms curled up
and glazed, the egress

like a trumpet. Some cones
with tight twisted sphincters

rugos and spiculate,
cactus-humped or warted,

others slick and simple
pods where tender jellies hid.

The frigid souls, the
amorphous ones, emptied

from out their skeletons
that were their furled caves.

Each an eccentric
mummy-case, one facet mute

and ultimate, one baffling
in its ruffles as a rose.

The largest, a valve of
bone streaked like a cloud,

its shadowy crease a pinched
ambiguous vestibule, a puckered

trap ajar: the sly inviting
smile into the labyrinth.

ANY OBJECT

any Object before the Eye
can fill the space can occupy
the supple frame of eternity

my Hand before me such
tangents reaches into Much
root and twig extremes can touch

any Hour can be the all
expanding like a cunning Ball
to a Vast from very small

skull and loin the twin-shaped Cup
store the glittering grainery up
for all the sandy stars to sup

any Single becomes the More
multiples sprout from alpha's core
from Vase of legend vessels of lore

to this pupil dark and wild
where lives the portrait of a Child
let me then be reconciled

germ of the first Intent to be
i am and must be seen to see
then every New descends from me

uncoiling into Motion i
start a massive panoply
the anamolecular atoms fly

and spread through ether like a foam
appropriating all the Dome
of absoluteness for my home

FOUNTAINS OF AIX

Beards of water
some of them have.
Others are blowing whistles of water.
Faces astonished that constant water
jumps from their mouths.
Jaws of lions are snarling water
through green teeth over chins of moss.
Dolphins toss jets of water
from open snouts
to an upper theater of water.
Children are riding swans and water
coils from the S-shaped necks and spills
in flat foils from pincered bills.
A solemn curly-headed bull
puts out a swollen tongue of water.
Cupids naked are making water
into a font that never is full.
A goddess is driving a chariot through water.
Her reins and whips are tight white water.
Bronze hoofs of horses wrangle with water.
Marble faces half hidden in leaves.
Faces whose hair is leaves and grapes
of stone are peering from living leaves.
Faces with mossy lips unlocked
always uttering water,
water
wearing their features blank
their ears deaf, their eyes mad
or patient or blind or astonished at water
always uttered out of their mouths.

WATERS

OCEAN, WHALE-SHAPED

Ocean, whale-shaped, rocking between the dunes,
in the gateway of their great naked knees,
horizon chafing a tame sky,

your vast back purple, your shoreward side
wallowing blue, fretted with racing foam,
green, then diamond your fin flashes on sand.

Glazed monuments of the wind, the dunes,
their sprawling limbs Olympian lift and fall
to slopes and platforms seeming hard as bone,

but footsteps scar their flanks like snow;
their white bodies shift,
are shunted by you, blue-black, boisterous whale —

and whittled, are rewhittled by the wind
unsatisfied with any shape or perpetuity.
The land, the sand we tread is not the steady

element our feet believe.
Indelible ocean, humped beside the sky,
you unsubstantial we can't grasp or walk on,

you pry at these gates and break them when you will —
overwhelming whale of water, mover and shaper,
over and over carving your cradle here.

THE SEA

When the sea is calm I wade
into her glossy swells
Their bloom of froth sways toward me
Like crossing a field where the grain
ripens ever higher
I would walk to the true center
leaving no furrow behind me
would walk down
in the secret shade
and hide like a child
by the motionless roots
of the tall tangled water

When the sea is wild
on her harsh pelt of sand the near waves
put fetlocks of foam on my ankles
An enormous bristling scroll
unwinds and rerolls frenzied white
at its edge icy green in its oncoming curl
Like the gap between lightning
and thunder a towering moment of dread
The great cavity
darkens to black
Then the smash
A monumental vase has broken on the beach

The sea retreats in a hissing
spate of silver raking sand and shells
and smooth-sucked stones into her pouch
And I am pulled forward
by the flashing magnet of the sea
outward toward her hungry to fall
into her rough insane
annihilating grasp

FROM SEA CLIFF, MARCH

The water's wide spread
(it is storm gray)
following the border of the far shore ahead,
leads the eye south,
tucks into a cove
where, at the point of another line of hills,
big rocks like huts
strung along the flats
are embraced by the sliding
long arms of the tide.
A red buoy bangs (but you can't hear it,
size of a golf tee seen from here),
wind is picking up, cleats of the water
rising and deepening, no white ridges yet.

In the cove's corner
on an island by itself,
an intricate old house,
set on a rock shelf
beside a lighthouse, saltcellar shaped,
with a round silvery top,
pokes up alone in the wind's main way.
Old house, of many chimneys, dormers and decks,
doll-sized, of clapboard, is outlined plain
at the farthest string of sight,
perched under swirling specks of white
gulls against gray
wide water, lowering sky
shutting down the distance under wind and rain.

STARING AT THE SEA ON THE DAY
OF THE DEATH OF ANOTHER

The long body of the water fills its hollow,
slowly rolls upon its side,
and in the swaddlings of the waves,
their shadowed hollows falling forward with the tide,

like folds of Grecian garments molded to cling
around some classic immemorial marble thing,
I see the vanished bodies of friends who have died.

Each form is furled into its hollow,
white in the dark curl,
the sea a mausoleum, with countless shelves,
cradling the prone effigies of our unearthly selves,

some of the hollows empty, long niches in the tide.
One of them is mine
and gliding forward, gaping wide.

THE PROMONTORY MOMENT

Think of only now, and how this pencil
tilted in the sand, might be a mast,
its shadow to an ant marking the sun's place.
Little and vast are the same to that big eye
that sees no shadow.

Think how future and past, afloat on an ocean
of breath, linked as one island,
might coexist with the promontory moment
around the sun's disc — for that wide eye
knows no distance or divide.

Over your shoulder in the circular cove, the sea,
woven by swimmers' gaudy heads, pulses an indigo
wing that pales at its frothy edge.
And, far out, sails as slow as clouds
change bodies as they come about.

Look at the standing gull, his pincered beak
yellow as this pencil, a scarlet streak beneath the tip,
the puff of his chest bowl-round and white,
his cuff-button eye of ice and jet
fixed on the slicing waves; shingle-snug, his gray wing
tucked to his side. Aloft, that plumpness,
whittled flat, sits like a kite.

Turn to where fishermen rise from a neck
of rock, rooted and still, rods played like spouts
from their hips. Until, beneath the chips of waves,
a cheek rips on the barb; a silver soul is flipped
from the sea's cool home into fatal air.

Close your eyes and hear the toss of the waves'
innumerable curls on the brow of the world.
That head is shaggy as Samson's, and three-fourths
furred. And *now* is eternal in beard and tress
piled green, blown white on churned sand,
the brand of the past an ephemeral smutch
of brown seaweed cast back to the sucking surf.

Tomorrow the marge is replaced
by a lace of shells, to be gathered again
by the hairy sea when it swells. Here nothing is built
or grown, and nothing destroyed. And the buoyed
mind dares to enmirror itself,
as the prone body, bared to the sun,
is undone of its cares.

The eye, also a sun, wanders,
and all that it sees it owns.

The filled sail, tacking the line between water
and sky, its mast as high as this pencil,
becomes the gull's dropped quill, and the fleece
of the wave, and the sea robin's arc
now stilled on the rock.

EARLY MORNING: CAPE COD

We wake to double blue:
an ocean without sail,
sky without a clue
of white.
Morning is a veil
sewn of only two
threads, one pale,
one bright.

royal blue and shy
iris, queen and king
colors of low
and high.
Then dips
a sickle wing,
we hear a hinged cry:
taut as from a sling

We bathe as if in ink,
but peacock-eyed and clear;
a roof of periwink
goes steep
into a bell of air
vacant to the brink.
Far as we can peer
is deep

downwhips
a taunting gull.
And now across our gaze
a snowy hull
appears;
triangles
along its stays
break out to windpulls.

With creaking shears
the bright
gulls cut the veil
in two,
and many a clue
on scalloped sail
dots with white
our double blue.

RUNNING ON THE SHORE

The sun is hot, the ocean cool. The waves
throw down their snowy heads. I run
under their hiss and boom, mine their wild
breath. Running the ledge where pipers
prod their awls into sand-crab holes,
my barefoot tracks their little prints cross
on wet slate. Circles of romping water swipe
and drag away our evidence. Running and
gone, running and gone, the casts of our feet.

My twin, my sprinting shadow on yellow shag,
wand of summer over my head, it seems
that we could run forever while the strong
waves crash. But sun takes its belly under.
Flashing above magnetic peaks of the ocean's
purple heave, the gannet climbs,
and turning, turns
to a black sword that drops,
hilt-down, to the deep.

CAPTAIN HOLM

I see Captain Holm
in yellow slicker,
right hand behind him
on the stick of the tiller,
feet in the well
of his orange Sailfish:
like a butterfly's
single wing, it slants
upright over the bay.
Captain Holm, our neighbor,
eighty years old,
thin and sclerotic,

can still fold
legs into the hull,
balance a bony buttock
on the shelf of the stern.
With a tug at the mainstay
he makes his sail trim up,
sniffs out whatever wind there is.
This raw day,
Captain Holm's alone,
his scrap of color
the only one
on the wide bay.
Winter sunset transfuses
that frail wing.

ST. AUGUSTINE-BY-THE-SEA

I

A sullen morning.
A long string,
with knots in it,
being pulled,
pelicans fly,
follow the leader
in fog, their line
the only horizon.
When the measuring
string is lost,
sea becomes sky.

2

Peak tide.
Ocean trying
to bury the land

again, again
slaughters
the surf-pierced
reefs, grinding
coarse, sifting
fine, the sand
salmon, like flesh.

3

On reddish sand
by the coquina
cliffs, noon sun
swallows my body.
I lie in the mouth
of a cannibal flower.
Wave after hissing
wave, the cold sea
climbs to me
to douse with green
glaze and fizz white,
the fiery flower's
appetite.

STONE GULLETS

Stone gullets among   Inrush   Feed   Backsuck and
The borders swallow   Outburst   Huge engorgements   Swallow
In gulps the sea   Tide crams jagged   Smacks snorts chuckups   Follow
In urgent thirst   Jaws the hollow   Insurge   Hollow
Gushing evacuations follow   Jetty it must   Outpush   Greed

215

HOW EVERYTHING HAPPENS
(BASED ON A STUDY OF THE WAVE)

happen.

to

up

stacking

is

something

When nothing is happening

When it happens

something

pulls

back

not

to

happen.

When   has happened.

pulling back   stacking up

happens

has happened   stacks up.

When it   something   nothing

pulls back while

Then nothing is happening.

happens.

and

forward

pushes

up

stacks

something

Then

AT FIRST, AT LAST

At first the dips are shallow,
the peaks ever higher.
Until at last the peaks

are lower.
The valleys deepen.
It is a wave

that mounts and recoils.
Coming then to shadows
on the slopes,

rifts in the concaves,
what is there to do
but lie open-eyed and love

the wave? The wave that gave us
high joys
never again to be matched,

and shall give us,
till it breaks,
oh what

surprises, releases, abysses?
To feel, to feel.
To be the implement

and the wound of feeling.
To lie open to feeling
on the exploding breast, the wave.

SWIMMERS

Tossed
by the muscular sea,
we are lost,
and glad to be lost
in troughs of rough

love. A bath in
laughter, our dive
into foam,
our upslide and float
on the surf of desire.

But sucked to the root
of the water-mountain —
immense —
about to tip upon us
the terror of total

delight —
we are towed,
helpless in its
swell, by hooks
of our hair;

then dangled, let go,
made to race —
as the wrestling chest
of the sea, itself
tangled, tumbles

in its own embrace.
Our limbs like eels
are water-boned,
our faces lost
to difference and

contour, as the lapping
crests.
They cease
their charge,
and rock us

in repeating hammocks
of the releasing
tide —
until supine we glide,
on cool green

smiles
of an exhaling
gladiator,
to the shore
of sleep.

WAKING FROM A NAP ON THE BEACH

Sounds like big rashers of bacon frying.
I look up from where I'm lying,
expecting to see stripes red and white.
My eyes drop shut,
stunned by the sun.
Now the foam is flame,
the long troughs charcoal, but
still it chuckles and sizzles, it burns
and burns, and never gets done.
The sea is that
fat.

BEGINNING TO SQUALL

A Buoy like a man in a red sou'wester
is uP to the toP of its Boots in the water
 leaning to warn a Blue Boat

   that, BoBBing and shrugging, is nodding "No,"
      till a strong wave comes and it shivers "Yes."
         The white and the green Boats are quiBBling, too.
            What is it they don't want to do?

The Bay goes on Bouncing anchor floats,
their colors tennis and tangerine.
Two ruffled gulls laughing are laughing gulls,
   a finial Pair on the gray Pilings.

   Now the Boats are Buttoning slickers on
      which resemBle little tents.
         The Buoy is jumPing uP and down
            showing a Black Belt stenciled "1."

A yellow Boat's last to lower sail
to wraP like a Bandage around the Boom.
   Blades are sharPening in the water
         that Brightens while the sky goes duller.

A HURRICANE AT SEA

Slowly a floor rises, almost becomes a wall.
Gently a ceiling slips down, nearly becomes a floor.
A floor with spots that stretch, as on a breathing
animal's hide. It rises again with a soft lurch.

The floor tilts, is curved, appears to be racing north
with a pattern of dents and dips
over slashes of dark. Now there are white lips,
widening on the wall

that stands up suddenly. The ceiling is all
rumpled, snarled, like a wet animal's fur.
The floor hardens, humps up like rock,
the side of a hill too slant to walk.

White teeth are bared where lazy lips swam.
The ceiling is the lid of a box about to slam.
Is this a real floor I walk? It's an angry spine
that shoots up over a chasm of seething

milk — cold, churned, shoving the stern around.
There's the groaning sound
of a caldron about to buckle, maybe break.
A blizzard of glass and lace

shivers over this dodging box.
It glides up the next high hissing alp — halts
on top. But the top turns hollow while the hollow spins.
I run down a slope and feel like twins,

one leg northeast, one west.
The planks pitch leeward, level an instant, then
rear back to a flat, stunned rest.
It's frightening, that vacant moment. I feel

the Floor beneath the floor reel,
while a thickening wilderness is shunted aft, under.
I'm in a bottle becalmed, but a mountain bloats
ahead, ready to thunder

on it. The floor is rushed into the pit.
Maybe there's no bottom to it.
I'm buried in a quarry, locked in a bucking
room — or bottle, or box — near cracking,

that's knocked about in a black,
enormous, heavy, quaking Room.
Is there a bottom to it? I'm glad not to have to know.
Boulders, canyon-high, smash down on the prow,

are shattered to snow, and shouldered off somehow.
Tossed out again on top. Topside bounced
like a top, to scoot the bumpy floor . . .
Out there, it's slicked to a plane almost, already,

though chopped with white to the far baseboard.
The ceiling is placing
itself right, getting steadier,
licking itself smooth. The keel

takes the next swollen hills along their backs —
like a little dog gripped
to a galloping horse — slipping
once in a while, but staying on.

OLD NO. 1

A shock to find you washed up on the beach,
old No. 1, looking like an iron whale,
or a blunt rocket. What a storm it took

to pull you from bottom, breaking the root
of the anchor. And what a wave, to roll
your solid ton, like a giant's thick and broken

pencil point, so far up the scoured beach.
You're dumped on a ridge of sedge the storm tide
harvested, big ring in your snout half buried,

rusted cone below your watermark scabby orange,
glazed black paintskin of belly and round
tabled top fouled with dull white gull droppings.

But you're still No. 1 — it's clearly stenciled
upon you — old Stove Pipe, old Opera Hat,
Bouncer in the Channel, Policeman of the Bay

all boats salute. Your colleague, nipple-headed
Big Red, No. 2, is out there swaying on today's
gentler tide like a jolly bottle, but

you, Black Butt, you're gone aground, down
past the count of ten, with a frowzy dead gull
upended in the sandy litter by your side.

ZERO
IN THE COVE

The waves have frozen
in their tracks and turned
to snow, and into ice

              the snow has turned, become
     the shore. Where in soft
                  summer sand burned by

    water flat, paralytic
                     breakers stand hurled
  into a ridge of ice. Ice
                   fattens about the poles
that told the tide.
                Their two shadows point

   out stiff behind them on a dead
            floor, thickened and too rough
    for light to glass,

         as if the moon were drained
   of power, and water
        were unknown. The cove

     is locked, a still
         chest. Depth itself has
        died with its
      reflection
       lost.

NOVEMBER NIGHT

Sky's face so old,
one eyeball loose,

fallen to the side,
the walleyed moon,

among the mouse-gray
waves, its squints

of mercury roll.
An aging face slips

its symmetry; lip
lags, lid droops.

Behind the horizon
the slide begins,

of a blind,
thick-furred tide:

rat-swells rip
and top each other,

gulp each other,
bloat, and scoot

pale vomit out
on a moonless shore.

OVERBOARD

What throws you out is what drags you in

What drags you in is what throws you

What throws you out is what drags

What drags is what throws you

What throws you drags

What drags throws

Throws drag

Thrags

Drags throw

What throws drags

What drags you throws

What throws is what drags you

What drags you in is what throws

What throws you out is what drags you

What drags you in is what throws you out

What throws you in is what drags you

What drags you out is what throws

What throws you out drags you

What drags throws you in

What throws drags you

Drags throw you

Thrags

THE WAVE AND THE DUNE

The wave-shaped dune is still.
Its curve does not break,
though it looks as if it will,

like the head of the dune-
shaped wave advancing,
its ridge strewn

with white shards flaking.
A sand-faced image of the wave
is always in the making.

Opposite the sea's rough glass
cove, the sand's smooth-whittled cave,
under the brow of grass,

is sunny and still. Rushing
to place its replica
on the shore, the sea is pushing

sketches of itself
incessantly into the foreground.
All the models smash upon the shelf,

but grain by grain the creeping sand
reerects their profiles
and makes them stand.

THE BLUE BOTTLE

"Go
to the other
shore
and return,"
I wrote
in a note
to the bottle,
and put it in it.
It kept it
dry.
I could see
through
the blue
bottle blue
notepaper
with blue ink
words.
The cork was tight.
It might
make it.
Blue wavelets let
it go,
began to
take it.
Oh,
it hobbled
beyond the jetty
rocks barnacled
and snailed.
It bobbled,
snagged
on a crag,
wagged
with its butt
end butted,
but sailed

so far that
its glass
had to pass
for glitter,
among glitters,
on the flat
glass
of the bay
and my
eye-
glass.
Baited
with
words
and weighted,
I thought,
"It will get away.
Get away
with it!" I
thought,
watching
the laps,
the lapse,
listening
to the lisp,
the lips
of the bay-
mouth
making shore,
making sure
every rock got
rounded
a little more
today,
every pebble
pounded,

brought
to ground
and rounded,
to be gritted
to a grain
someday,
some sum-day
to be mounded
into rock again.
Some fishermen
were fishing
with little
fishes hooked
to hook
bigger fish.
And some they caught
and cooked.
And some they
put on bigger
hooks to get
bigger fishes yet.
And all day
the bay
smacked
its lips, big
and little,
rocking big and
little ships,
that smacked
and rocked like
oyster crackers
in a dish.
The tide
was either going
out or it
was coming in.

Not for an in-
stant could it stop,
since its pulse
compels
it, and since
the syndrome swells.
Since syn-rhythm
rules all motion,
and motion makes
erosion,
all that's munched
apart and
swallowed
shifts, collects, is
heaped and hollowed,
heaped and
hollowed, heaped
and hollowed.
All
the little
waves I
followed
out to where my
bottle wallowed.
I was sure, sure, sure,
I was shore,
shore it would endure,
endure,
would obey, obey
internal pulsion,
pulsion
of the bay,
would turn, turn,
return, return
with the turn-

turn-turn-
ing glassy floor
that bore
it, for
it wore
internal or-
der at its core.
Constantly
my eye
did pass
over blue,
looking
with blue,
for bluer
blue
on the bottle-
blue bay-glass.
When tide re-
turned,
when shore re-
stored,
my bottle's envelope
of glass
would
be re-
versed,
even though
its core
burst.
First
erosion,
then corrosion,
then assemblage.
It would be
nursed

again to
vessel-shape,
transparent float,
hard, hollow
bladder,
transferred
transplant,
holder of my note.
In what
language, then,
the words,
the words within
its throat?
What answer?
What other-colored
ink?
My blue
eye,
thinking,
thinking, blinked.
My
eye, my
I
lost link
with the blue
chink,
with crinkled
wavelets-lets-lets
let it, rising,
racing, wrinkling,
falling,
be swallowed
in that inkling,
let it
sink.

THE STICK

The stick is subject to the waves. The waves are subject to
the sea. The sea is subject to its frame. And that
is fixed, or seems to be.

What is it that the stick can do? Can tell the sky, "I
dip, I float. When a wave runs under me, I pretend
I am a boat. And the steersman and
the crew, and the cargo, compass, map. With
a notion of the shore,
I carry all within my lap."

And when a wave runs over it, what is it that the
stick decides? "From your bottom,
cruel sea, you have torn me with your
tides. I am a sliver from some boat, once
swallowed to its water-deep. Why
am I shifted, broken, lost? Let me down, my
rest to keep."

The sea is subject to its frame.
The waves are subject to the sea. The
stick is subject to the waves.
Or does it only seem to be?

What if the stick be washed ashore,
and, gnawed by wind, scoured
by sand, be taken up with other
sticks, into a hand? On some
predicated day, here is what
the stick might say:

"Inside my border, a green
sea flows, that while it
flows is still. A white
wall is around me,
where I am fixed by

someone's will,
who made my shape
into a frame,
and in
this corner
drew
his
name."

THE EVEN SEA

Meekly the sea
now plods to shore:
white-faced cattle used to their yard,
the waves, with weary knees,
come back from bouldered hills
of high water,

where all the gray, rough day they seethed like bulls,
till the wind laid down its goads
at shift of tide, and sundown
gentled them; with lowered necks
they amble up the beach
as to their stalls.

THE TIDE AT LONG POINT

The sea comes up and the sun goes over
    The sea goes out and the sun falls
The stubby shadow of the lighthouse pales
    stretches to a finger and inches east
The wind lifts from off the sea
    and curries and curries the manes of the dunes

The pipers and the terns skate over
     tweaking the air with their talk
In sky clean as a cat-licked dish
     clouds are sandbars bared by ebbing blue

The hourglass is reversed

The sea comes up and the moon peers over
     The sea goes out and the moon swells
The shadow of the lighthouse thick as a boot
     is swiped by a whiskered beam
The wind licks at the jetty stones
     The pipers and terns hunch on the spit
hiding their necks and stilted feet
     The sky has caught a netful of stars
The moon is a dory trolling them in

The hourglass is reversed

The sea comes up and the moon tips under
     The sea goes out and the sun looms
The sun is a schooner making for harbor
     Shallops of cloud are adrift in the west
The wind gallops the waves to a lather
     and lashes the grass that shines on the dunes
The lighthouse looks at its twin in the water
     The pipers and terns preen on its brow

A F T E R P I E C E

INCANTATION

Bright sleep bathing breathing walking
snow ocean and fire
spinning white and flinching green
red-and-yellow-petaled sheen
color me with fresh desire

Vast sleep snow as deep
fresh the leap to green and steep flinching wave
pulsing red glowers flow on black below

In black sleep brightness keep
in colored day spin and play
fresh foam sharp snow the slime of time whirl away
Fire is air is breath and green
lakes of air I walking swim

Powers are of motion made
of color braided all desire
In red and yellow flowers bathe
in snow ocean and fire
in snowy sleep on curls of flame
on shingles of the sea I climb
Dim and gray whirl away and knotted thought and slime

Burning snow spin me so with black sea
to braided be   In green sleep eons leap
from gray slime past thought and time
to pith and power to bathe in the immortal hour
to breathe from another pulsing flower

Snow ocean white fire
color me with fresh desire

INDEX OF TITLES

May Swenson kept a master index in which she noted publication information as well as the date she began each poem. Those dates follow the poems listed here. In the absence of a beginning date, the publication date is given.

Above Bear Lake (8/73), p. 120
Above the Arno (8/21/60), p. 46
After the Flight of Ranger 7 (8/3/64),
    p. 179
All That Time (6/3/63), p. 163
Almanac (5/56), p. 31
Alternate Hosts (10/52), p. 149
Alyscamps at Arles, The (7/1/60),
    p. 75
Angels at "Unsubdued" (6/4/77),
    p. 108
Another Spring Uncovered
    (3/24/59), p. 123
Any Object (1952), p. 202
April Light (4/61), p. 87
As Long Ago As Far Away (2/58),
    p. 185
At First, at Last (11/1/63), p. 217
At Truro (8/14/64), p. 54

Beast (1933), p. 25
Beauty of the Head, The (6/70), p. 37
Beginning to Squall (10/3/67), p. 219
Big-Hipped Nature (7/52), p. 160

Birthday (8/25/70), p. 45
Bison Crossing Near Mt. Rushmore
    (Summer 1973), p. 158
Bleeding (4/16/68), p. 64
Blue (4/1/67), p. 29
Blue Bottle, The (10/24/67), p. 227
Bronco Busting, Event #1
    (Winter 1973), p. 154
By Morning (1952), p. 193

Cabala (8/61), p. 23
Camoufleur (1/23/69), p. 108
Camping in Madera Canyon
    (3/74), p. 118
Captain Holm (2/25/76), p. 213
Catbird in Redbud (4/27/67), p. 96
Centaur, The (12/54), p. 13
City Garden in April, A (4/16/65),
    p. 88
Cloud-Mobile, The (7/9/57), p. 174
Come In Go Out (9/12/77), p. 3
Comet Watch on Indian Key —
    Night of April 10, 1986 (4/10/86),
    p. 182

Couple, A (6/58), p. 150
Crossing, The (8/57), p. 17
Cumuli (7/52), p. 175

Daffodildo (5/2/64), p. 41
Day Is Laid By, A (1935), p. 4
Day Like Rousseau's *Dream*, A
   (Winter 1979), p. 85
Day Moon, The (9/57), p. 173
Dear Elizabeth (9/17/63), p. 133
Death, Great Smoothener (1954),
   p. 80
Death Invited (6/4/60), p. 158
Deciding (1954), p. 36
Digging in the Garden of Age I Un-
   cover a Live Root (9/12/77), p. 60
Downward (1961), p. 68
Dream, A (1951), p. 21
Dream After Nanook (2/57), p. 142

Each Like a Leaf (2/62), p. 161
Early Morning: Cape Cod (7/53),
   p. 212
Earth Your Dancing Place (1936),
   p. 16
Engagement, The (2/55), p. 82
Even Sea, The (7/53), p. 230
Evolution (3/49), p. 27
Exchange, The (8/6/61), p. 8

Fable for When There's No Way Out
   (7/25/65), p. 151
Feel Like a Bird (3/49), p. 124
Feel Me (3/4/64), p. 79
Flag of Summer (7/58), p. 100
Fluffy Stuff, The (1/84), p. 65
Flying Home from Utah (9/62),
   p. 175

Forest (8/5/56), p. 34
Fountain Piece (9/55), p. 112
Fountains of Aix (7/60), p. 203
From Sea Cliff, March (3/9/76),
   p. 209

Garden at St. John's, The (1951),
   p. 196
Gods | Children (6/17/63), p. 164
Goodbye, Goldeneye (11/17/82),
   p. 117
Goodnight (1934), p. 143
Green Red Brown and White (9/50),
   p. 32

Haymaking (7/36), p. 100
Hearing the Wind at Night (6/10/63),
   p. 65
Her Management (9/57), p. 102
Horse (1970s), p. 63
How Everything Happens (10/1/67),
   p. 216
How to Be Old (10/23/60), p. 6
Hurricane at Sea, A (11/60), p. 220

If I Had Children (12/16/81), p. 20
I Look at My Hand (3/12/61), p. 19
Incantation (1952), p. 235
In the Bodies of Words (8/15/79),
   p. 135
In the Yard (6/5/67), p. 94
I Will Lie Down (1939), p. 71

Lake Scene, A (8/56), p. 12
Landing on the Moon (2/58), p. 177
Laocoön Dream Recorded in
   Diary Dated 1943 (8/51), p. 22
Last Day (12/31/86), p. 81

Lightning, The (4/19/63), p. 50

Little Rapids, The (1953 or 1959),
  p. 68

Living Tenderly (6/10/62), p. 3

Loaf of Time, A (9/51), p. 33

Look Closer (3/29/88), p. 191

Love Sleeping (n.d.), p. 28

Lying and Looking (n.d.), p. 30

Manyone Flying (12/30/75), p. 49

Mornings Innocent (6/49), p. 26

Motherhood (11/30/62), p. 155

My Farm (2/59), p. 140

Naked in Borneo (10/12/63), p. 138

Nature (6/23/71), p. 78

Navajo Blanket, A (Winter 1974–75),
  p. 192

New Pair, A (9/30/85), p. 122

News from the Cabin (10/57), p. 147

North Rim, The (Summer 1971),
  p. 194

November Night (11/27/72), p. 224

Ocean, Whale-Shaped (8/54), p. 207

October (8/18/75), p. 55

October Textures (10/12/64), p. 121

Of Rounds (1/58), p. 180

Old No. 1 (3/18/76), p. 222

On Addy Road (Spring 1974), p. 107

Once There Were Glaciers (n.d.),
  171

One Morning in New Hampshire
  (8/56), p. 97

One of the Strangest (1/72), p. 113

On Handling Some Small Shells
  from the Windward Islands
  (6/4/65), p. 199

On Its Way (10/69), p. 5

On the Edge (4/15/69), p. 51

Orbiter 5 Shows How Earth Looks
  from the Moon (8/14/67), p. 178

Order of Diet (8/56), p. 74

Out of the Sea, Early (8/17/64),
  p. 164

Overboard (11/10/69), p. 225

Pair, A (4/17/68), p. 116

Picasso: "Dream." Oil. 1932
  (12/31/68), p. 138

Pigeon Woman (8/6/59), p. 114

Playhouse, The (7/52), p. 131

Poplar's Shadow, The (11/54),
  p. 18

Process, The (1954), p. 168

Promontory Moment, The
  (7/55), p. 210

Question (1954), p. 45

Rain at Wildwood (5/28/65), p. 94

Red Bird Tapestry, The (12/55),
  p. 141

Running on the Shore (9/18/71),
  p. 213

Rusty Autumn (9/50), p. 70

Scroppo's Dog (9/9/74), p. 61

Sea, The (1941), p. 208

Secure (1941), p. 71

Seeing Jupiter (5/8/69), p. 183

Shu Swamp, Spring (4/1/73), p. 96

Sketch for a Landscape (1940), p. 99

Skopus (n.d.), p. 186

Sleeping Overnight on the Shore
  (9/9/63), p. 171

Snow Geese at Jamaica Bay, The
   (4/23/62), p. 113
Snowy, The (9/88), p. 110
Solar Corona, The (1974), p. 184
Speed (7/26/70), p. 196
Spring by Robert Lowell (Photograph
   by Trudi Fuller) (2/14/67), p. 137
Spring Uncovered (4/57), p. 86
Staring at the Sea on the Day of the
   Death of Another (12/72), p. 210
St. Augustine-by-the-Sea (12/71),
   p. 214
Stick, The (2/19/68), p. 229
Still Turning (8/16/64), p. 72
Stone Gullets (10/68), p. 215
Stripping and Putting On (9/7/63),
   p. 126
Subconscious Sea (n.d.), p. 69
Subject of the Waves, A (10/20/67),
   p. 52
Summer's Bounty (7/9/85), p. 102
Sunday in the Country (1950), p. 24
Surface, The (8/61), p. 198
Survey of the Whole (4/1/70),
   p. 187
Swimmers (7/15/58), p. 218

Thickening Mat, The (1/25/71),
   p. 35
This Morning (1/17/70), p. 60

Tide at Long Point, The (8/54),
   p. 230
Tree in Spring, A (4/25/89), p. 93
Trinity Churchyard, Spring 1961
   (10/61), p. 77
Truth Is Forced, The (3/16/61), p. 11

Untitled (6/10/66), p. 4

View to the North (10/18/74), p. 7

Waking from a Nap on the Beach
   (8/13/64), p. 219
Waterbird (1971), p. 122
Water Picture (2/28/55), p. 92
Wave and the Dune, The (8/7/64),
   p. 226
Weather (6/15/62), p. 66
Wednesday at the Waldorf (4/6/67),
   p. 157
What I Did on a Rainy Day (10/51),
   p. 30
Willets, The (5/10/70), p. 117
Woods at Night, The (4/28/62),
   p. 109

Yes, the Mystery (n.d.), p. 67

Zambesi and Ranee (11/55), p. 152
Zero in the Cove (1/16/68), p. 223

ABOUT THE POET

May Swenson was born on May 28, 1913, in Logan, Utah, and died on December 4, 1989, in Ocean View, Delaware. In that lifetime she worked as a newspaper reporter, ghostwriter, editor, secretary, manuscript reader for New Directions, and poet-in-residence, but always and mainly as a poet. Eleven volumes of her poetry were published during her lifetime. These earned for her much praise from fellow poets, a place in the hearts and minds of poetry lovers, and many awards, among them the Brandeis University Creative Arts Award, Rockefeller, Guggenheim, and Ford fellowships, the Bollingen Prize for Poetry, a grant from the National Endowment for the Arts, an honorary doctor of letters degree from Utah State University, and a MacArthur Fellowship. She was a member of the American Academy and Institute of Arts and Letters and a chancellor of the Academy of American Poets.